The Book of
Easton

The Book of
Easton

Memories of Cardinal
Adam de Easton's Birthplace

Easton Village History Project

HALSGROVE

First published in Great Britain in 2004

British Library Cataloguing-in-Publication Data
A CIP record for this title is available from the British Library

ISBN 1 84114 339 1

HALSGROVE

Halsgrove House
Lower Moor Way
Tiverton, Devon EX16 6SS
Tel: 01884 243242
Fax: 01884 243325
E-mail: sales@halsgrove.co.uk
Website: www.halsgrove.co.uk

Frontispiece: *The Dog public house, 1920s.*

Printed and bound in Great Britain by CPI Bath

Contents

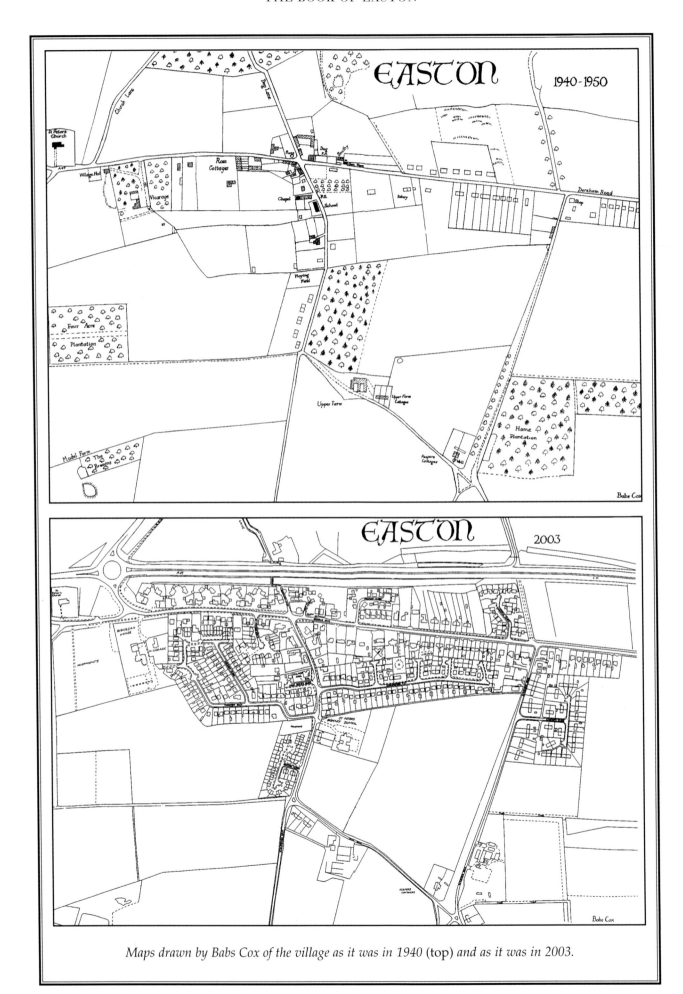

Maps drawn by Babs Cox of the village as it was in 1940 (top) and as it was in 2003.

Acknowledgements

The Easton Village History Project Committee would like to thank all those who have assisted in the compilation of this book. Although too many to name individually, there are those that deserve a special mention: Babs Cox for drawing the maps of Easton, past and present; Dave Ditton for his photography; the school for delving into their archives and loaning us books and photographs; the people who have left the village but still supplied us with information; the loan of information already gathered by John Rampton; Ada Mouat for her contribution and Jean Ditton and Merilyn Cossey for typing the text. Thanks are also due to the *Eastern Evening News* for the loan of six photographs used in the book.

Fancy dress in the village, early 1930s.

Mr King's shop, late 1800s.

Above: *Group of children, 1960s.* Left to right: *Trevor McCadden, William Garnet, Roy Bargewell, Alan Bargewell, Stephen Peacock.*

Right: *The Chapman family: Tom and Blanche with,* left to right, *Raymond, baby, Royston and Roland in 1914.*

Below: *Mr Kenny Cossey (on the right), who is pictured with his young son Heriot and his farm horses, Captain and Major, early 1940s. Philip Welles is on the left.*

Introduction

This project was born in the year 2000 when Age Concern introduced the idea of a history project entitled 'Your Village'. The Good Companions formed a committee to take the idea further. Daunted by the seeming enormity of the task, we were very lucky to have someone take us under their wing to produce an audio CD. Our luck continued and we received a Millennium Award for the CD and all went ahead. With about a dozen villagers contributing thoughts and memories of life in Easton through the years, the CD represented an hour of real entertainment.

In the wake of its success, our confidence grew and we decided to go ahead and produce a book. We had so many lovely pictures of the village, past and present, and so many memories from people who have lived here like their ancestors before them. We all hope that you enjoy our stories and reminiscences and that this project perhaps gives others the confidence to research the history of their own village or parish.

The Committee consists of Merilyn Cossey, chairman; Thelma Kidd, treasurer; Jean Ditton, secretary and the Millennium Award winner and producer of the audio CD; Joan Chapman; Pat Wiepen; Hazel Harrowven; Revd Angela Reynolds and Bertie Sparkes. We all enjoyed the work involved in producing *The Book of Easton* and had many a laugh at the tales that were told.

Easton Village History Project Committee.
Left to right, back row: *Merilyn Cossey, Pat Wiepen, Thelma Kidd, Revd Angela Reynolds, Jean Ditton;*
front row: *Joan Chapman, Bertie Sparkes, Hazel Harrowven.*

Left: The *village sign with its representation of Adam de Easton, and the village pump.*

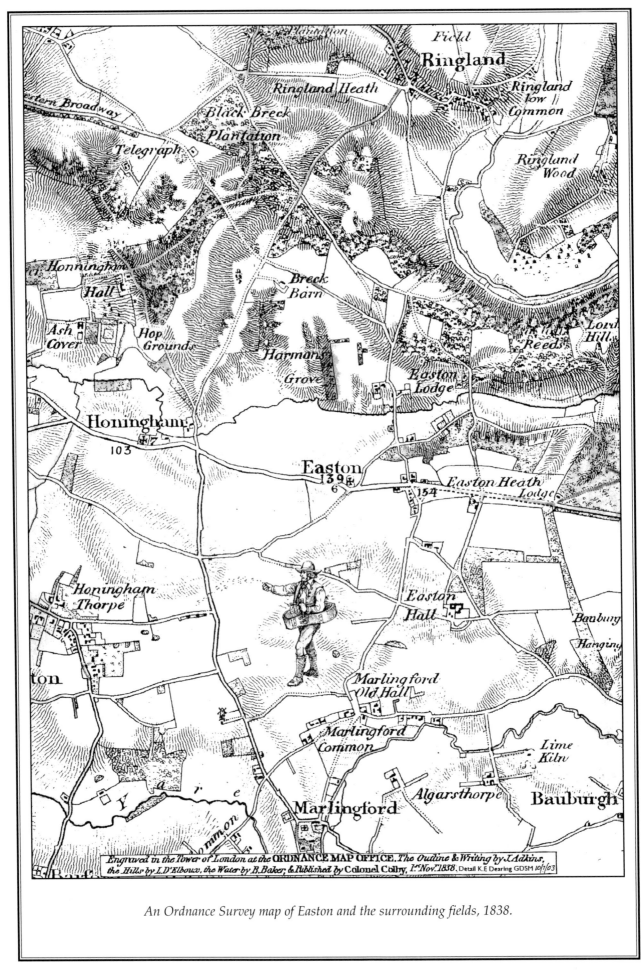

An Ordnance Survey map of Easton and the surrounding fields, 1838.

Chapter One

❧

Early History

Easton lies six miles west of Norwich on the A47. Surrounded mostly by arable farmland, it is the home of Easton College. The Roman road which ran from Caister to the west of the county, and beyond to the coast of Lynn, took Roman traders and troops through the parish around 1,500 years ago, and various remains from the period have been discovered here.

The earliest documented records tell us that by the seventh century AD a settlement had been established at this place. It was called Estuna, or East-Town, 'Est' referring to its situation from Hingham, the head town of the Deanery, and 'Ton' the Anglo-Saxon word for a tract of land enjoyed by a community. In 1086, William the Conqueror's men arrived to take details for the Domesday Book Estuna. Easton is listed as follows:

Lands of Count Alan, Bawburgh is 5 furlongs in length and 4 in breadth and pays 8½d in geld and (Honingham) Thorpe is 5 furlongs in length and 4 in breadth and (pays) 6½d in geld. And the land of the sokeman is 6 furlongs in length and 5 in breadth and (pays) 13½d in geld. Easton (near Norwich) and Honingham which a certain one of these sokeman holds is 6 furlongs in length and 5 in breadth.

The Count Alan was Earl Alan Richmond of the manor of Cossey. He had 144 men under him in the manorial system, seven of whom lived in Barford, Estuna and Honingham. They paid geld (as we pay taxes) and did not own their land but held it with the obligation of serving their overlord when called upon. The Earl, in turn, vowed allegiance to the King. It was a military overlordship, and aristocracy was geared to war. Practically all the overlords were Norman-French nobles who had come over to England with William the Conqueror.

It is thought that a Saxon church still stood in the village in 1150, and was called St Mary's (which is now the Lady chapel) – with the small tower erected in the west end being used as a watch-tower for the area. Estuna was on the road from the 'new' shrine of Herbert de Losinga at Norwich Cathedral and the 'old' shrine of St Withburga in East Dereham, so many pilgrims rested here and said prayers at the church.

Adam de Easton, the cardinal depicted on the village sign (at the corner of Dog Lane and the turn-pike road, now the Dereham Road), was born in 1330; he was descended from an ancient family of landowners living at Easton and Honingham.

The plague of 1348–49 hit East Anglia hard, with a terrible loss of life; in this area more than half of the population perished – a considerably higher proportion than was the case elsewhere in the country. Those who did survive in Easton – and they were very few – moved from the little East Chapel on the main road down to the stream (ford) at Lower Easton where new cottages were built to house them.

During the period 1649–60 Easton briefly became quite well known. In 1650 the village set the scene for one of the most bitter and well-remembered tragedies of the time. The struggle was between those that followed the King (the Royalists) and those who followed Cromwell (the Parliamentarians). Norwich, and much of Norfolk, had quickly fallen to the Cromwellians, and so the families that remained loyal to the King generally kept a very low profile. A meeting was arranged in December on Easton Heath at which the Royalists assembled to begin their march on Norwich. The siege failed and all who were involved were hanged, some in their own villages.

St Peter's Church, 2004.

*The Church of
Santa Cecilia in Rome.*

Left: *The tomb of Adam de Easton in Rome.*

Below: *Adam de Easton's effigy on his tomb in Rome.*

Chapter Two

❧

Cardinal and Church

Cardinal Adam de Easton

by Jean Ditton

Adam was born in Easton in 1330 and is descended from an ancient family of landowners from Easton and Honingham. His tomb can be found in the ancient church of Santa Cecilia in Trastevere in Rome, built during the third and fifth centuries. The following is an outline account of his life:

Cardinal, born at Easton in Norfolk; died in Rome, 15 September (according to others, 20 October) 1397. He joined the Benedictines at Norwich. He probably accompanied Archbishop Langham to Rome and, being a man of learning and ability, obtained a post in the Curia. He was made Cardinal-priest of the title of St. Celia by Urban 6th, probably in December 1381. On 7th March 1381 or 1382, he was nominated Dean of York. In 1385 he was imprisoned by Urban on a charge of conspiring with five other Cardinals against the Pope and was deprived of his Cardinalate and deanery. The next Pope, Boniface 9th, restored his Cardinalate 18th December 1389 and for a time Adam returned to England, where he held a prebend in Salisbury Cathedral, which he subsequently exchanged for the living of Heygham in Norwich. He wrote many works, none of which are extant, and is stated to have composed the Office for the Visitation of Our Lady.

Cardinal Adam de Easton on the village sign.

My sister was in Easton on holiday having come from Italy, where she has lived for the last 43 years, and she made a note to investigate our cardinal in more depth upon her return. I subsequently received a phone call from her to say that her husband Angelo had contacted the church priest and explained about Adam. They were told that they would be allowed to take some photographs for me. Both of them went to Rome and took some wonderful pictures, and I am so thrilled that we now know where our cardinal is buried. On the tomb these words appear in Latin:

Adam from England. TTS Priest of Caecillae's Church Ecclesiastical Cardinal in the district of Pope Leo 4th Distinguished administrator of integrity in doctrine and religion.

The Church of Our Lady and St Peter

The church is situated at the west end of the village, alongside the old A47. It has a wall at the front of the churchyard and wrought-iron gates. The following information is based on research carried out by the vicar, Roger Burt, in 1981.

It is thought that there has been a church in the village since the twelfth century, from which period both the tower arch and the south doorway are thought to date – and there is a plaque on the front of the church dated 1108; the (thatched) building at this time would probably have consisted of little more than a squat square west tower, a long narrow nave and a semi-circular apse at the east end. The then unglazed windows would have been quite narrow openings with semi-circular tops, they would have let in maximum light and a minimal amount of water.

Alterations to the church began in the thirteenth century, continuing into the fourteenth, and the present nave and chancel were added at this time, as also was the early-English lancet window at the east end of the Lady chapel. An example of the beautiful tracery work of the Decorated period can be seen in the west window. The font is thirteenth-century Purbeck marble, with two shallow arches on each face, and rests on several pillars as are typical for the date. The fourteenth century also saw the birth of Adam of Easton, the cardinal on our village sign.

The church probably reached its peak of development during the fifteenth century. All the windows were replaced in what is known as the Perpendicular style and the clerestory windows in the nave give a particularly impressive light to the whole. The south porch is probably of this period, with a brick frame around the outer door. Some of the buttresses were also added at this time.

During the sixteenth century the building was allowed to fall into disrepair as the new patrons were Roman Catholics. Thus, by the seventeenth century it was noted that at:

... Easton – the glasse wyndowes on the sowth syde of

the church are much decayed, wch cannott yet well be repeyred, by reason on the rooffe of the church on that syde was of late utterly fallen downe...

There was one small improvement in the 1600s, however, as the porch sundial was added in 1697.

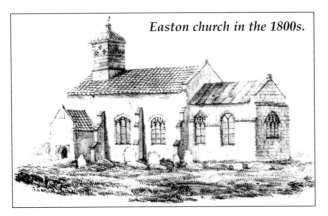

Easton church in the 1800s.

The year 1778 saw a 'great gale' which may have been partly responsible for the collapse of the tower and the concomitant destruction of the west end of the church, along with three bells. These latter were sold and the money was given towards the purchase of a new bell and the cupola. Mural paintings were discovered depicting the martyrdom of St Thomas à Becket of Canterbury, but these were not preserved. Pilgrims on their way to Walsingham used the church as a chapel.

During the early years of Queen Victoria's reign church life was at a very low ebb, and the fabric, walls and roof had fallen into decay. But with the revival of the Oxford Movement in the 1850s there came an increasing keenness to restore and refurbish; and a large amount of what we presently have is due to the devotion of the period. Outside, the bell cupola was removed and replaced by a bell cote in 1848. The pitch of the north aisle roof was raised, but this effectively cut the attractive Perpendicular clerestory windows in half; the effect of the alteration can clearly be seen inside. The base of the tower was turned into a storeroom, and extensive restorations were carried out to the chancel (1883–84) to the tune of £450. The external walls were resurfaced with flints, and new coping and a floriated cross were added, with the chancel being given a new slate roof. Inside, the old rood-screen was removed, the chancel arch was rebuilt, the chancel floor was re-laid and choir-stalls were built. The music gallery was dismantled, and part of this was made into a screen dividing the ancient Church of Our Lady (the Lady chapel) from the nave.

The early-twentieth century saw the Reserved Sacrament being reintroduced, and set in a tabernacle in the Lady chapel together with a sanctuary lamp and incense, setting quite a different scene to that experienced during the early-Victorian years. Two white plaster statues, one of Our Lord, the other of Our Lady, were introduced, as well as wrought-iron riddle posts, and gold curtains around the altar.

Easton church in the early 1900s.

Far left: *William Harrowven with his bicycle, early 1930s.*

Left: *The plaque on the wall of the church commemorating the men killed in the First World War.*

Bottom: *Bob Harrowven's baptism certificate, early 1930s.*

The first vicar to live in the village was the Revd Warren Blake (in 1882) and it was for him that the Vicarage was built. He spent his early years doing what he could to restore part of the church. The patron at that time was Robert Fellowes. A gifted musician, Revd Blake settled at the Vicarage and soon had a carriage and pair with coachman, two gardeners and two maids at his service. He retired in 1914 and was followed by Revd W.E. Perrin, who restored the north aisle. He was very High Church (Anglo-Catholic) and thought the world of his little church, keeping it spotlessly clean and the sanctuary lamp always burning in the chancel. With help he hung a large crucifix in the chancel arch. Mrs Perrin, meanwhile, ran the Sunday school and played the ancient organ, which because if its antiquity was known as the 'Wheeze-e Anna' – it rattled and groaned when blown by a village boy. It finally collapsed in 1927 when a new one was obtained, which is still used at the time of writing. Revd Perrin left the village in 1928.

Revd B. Pugh took his place. Low Church, he was a marked contrast to his predecessor but had a good following. He restored the nave and with a band of willing helpers raised the money to restore half of the roof. He did not stay long, however, and left in 1932.

Next came Revd Frank Bracecampe, a moderate churchman who appealed to most of the men in the parish. Unlike his predecessors he was not dependent on the annual wage. He continued the restoration work, finishing the rest of the roof, relining the windows with lead, removing the screen and refitting it across the west end of the nave. He was also very musical and founded and trained the choir of eight men, ten boys and four ladies, all robed in purple cassocks and surplices. The Sunday school was very large and had splendid equipment. Many more alterations were done to the church and he had the Church Room doubled in size with the addition of a cloakroom and kitchen. In the Vicarage he had a bathroom and an extra bedroom, and new drainage and electric light were installed. He left Easton in 1936 to go to Ormesby St Mary, Great Yarmouth. There are some villagers still living in Easton who remember him as being a friend of travellers and he would often go on walks from village to village with them.

In 1937 the Revd John Oswald Dean became the new vicar. He was a young man with plenty of pep and had a wonderful voice. He did an enormous amount of good work in the parish in the few years that he was here, continuing to work with and greatly

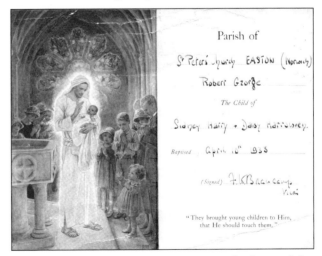

The Revd Bracecampe.

improve the choir. The new vestry at the base of the tower (this was an old coke store) was restored by him and many volunteer labourers. New cupboards and vestments were built and given by Clifford King, associate of the present-day Wallace Kings Furnishers. A new heating system with boilers and six radiators as well as electricity were installed. The Revd John Dean was very popular and is talked about, even today. He is remembered particularly for his kindness. A letter from Mr Ron Greenacre, who was born in the village in 1925, gives us a lovely report of him:

The Revd Dean visited the church school regularly and also ran the Sunday school. I still have three books of Charles Dickens stories awarded to me as prizes and all signed by him. I was particularly grateful to him when I broke my leg. At that time I was attending the CNS School (City Norwich School) and was in plaster for 9 months. During that period he obtained the curriculum from the school. I managed to get to the Vicarage on my crutches and he gave me the necessary tuition and homework. As a result I did not drop a class and my only failure was French.

Another two memories also came back. One was after taking the 11-plus exam I had to have an interview at the Education Office in Norwich, he offered to take me. He had a Wolsey Saloon Car – one of the best in those days – and on the way home reached 100mph between the Roundwell and Easton Church – to me this was obviously a great thrill. The second was when he visited me at home with my broken leg; he asked my mother if there was anything I wanted and she said that I had been asking for bananas. At lunchtime a boy called from the school with a bunch of bananas from him. Mrs Dean was an ex actress and gave us instruction in the nativity play. I was one of the three kings...

Mrs Amy M. Scarfe also recalled this production, writing, in a letter to her sister-in-law:

The play was a huge success – we thought it lovely. The dresses and colouring was grand. The angels were sweet in their silver and white. The children played it well. Mrs Dean was delighted with the success of it. The photograph and account of it is in this week's press.

Nativity play, 1939. Left to right, back: Angel Heather Sherwood, Mary is played by Cissie Spooner, small angel by Mollie Mortimer, Joseph by Arnold Walpole, small angel by Irene Mortimer, big angel by Barbara McCadden; front: shepherds are Teddy Pratt, Brian Markham and Joan Gent; two small children: Dolly Harrowven and Bertie Sparkes, and the three Kings are Peter Scarfe, Ronnie Greenacre and Paul Markham.

Revd Dean was indeed wonderful with the children and sorted out both the football club and the youth club.

He joined up in 1939 as a Royal Army chaplain with the Royal Norfolks. Mrs Dean and her maid Elsie Farmer took on the Sunday school and many other duties in his absence. Revd John Dean was taken prisoner in Singapore and later placed in Changi Jail. We have a report from a George Clapham who was with him as a POW; he said that he was always comforting the sick and wounded. He contracted beriberi and died on 16 April 1942 aged 35. A letter from Mr J.N. Farrow of Sheringham (also a POW), dated 1974, notes that he was with 'Padre Dean' at the time of his death and that he was buried on the afternoon of 18 April. Mr Farrow wrote: 'I carried the pass flag in front of a large parade of men who attended his funeral [the pass flag to get by the Japanese guards] on route to the cemetery.' Because Revd Dean's death was not known about until 1945, the Revd Jolly of Hockering and Revd T. Frost, the vicar of Bawburgh, kept the congregation and children together until the appointment of the Revd Colwell-Smith in 1946.

After the war the Revd Colwell-Smith came from Bungay and it was also at this time that the parish of Colton was joined with Easton. Revd Colwell-Smith was older than Revd Dean and had been a missionary in Burma. As was the case in most parishes after the war the congregation fell away and

Revd Dean in his Army uniform, 1940.

Confirmation at the church during Revd Dean's time, 1940. Left to right: Daphne Spooner, Bessie Bugg, Evelyn Spooner, Betty Mortimer, Beryl Mortimer, Heather Sherwood, Joan Gent.

Left: *Pat and Theo Wiepen's wedding in 1947 outside the church gates.*

the choir slowly vanished. The new vicar was an ill man and sadly died in Norwich in 1952. Details survive relating to a wedding which took place at the church during his incumbency:

We had fixed a date to be married but things did not go quite as planned right from the start. First the Vicar forgot to read the banns and we had to be married a week later and on the day there was thick fog all day. The Vicar conducted the service with his cassock tucked up the back of his neck. Then coming down from the altar we did not walk down the aisle but took a short cut around the chairs to the Vestry. When it came to signing the register he had forgotten a stamp to put on the certificate, which meant the guests in church had to be asked if any one had a postage stamp. Only one person did. That was Charlie Hart and it happened to be a tupenny hapenny one.

Revd Frank Jolly came to us from Liverpool in 1952. Some people knew of him already, his father having served as the vicar of Hockering many years earlier and he himself having filled the post of vicar of Costessey and Taverham before the Second World War. Frank Jolly was responsible for decorating the church with coloured paint and making some alterations in the building. There was a beautiful carpet laid in the chancel which had only been down a few months when it was stolen with a very old chest reputedly containing a silver chalice, books and some papers.

Mrs Jolly had a very good Sunday school and was also the organist, and together the couple started the Mothers' Union in the village which was very well attended. The members bought a royal-blue banner with Mary and Baby Jesus embroidered in gold, which was quite an achievement in those days. It would be taken to special church and cathedral services and carried in procession by Alice Sparkes, with Doris Peacock and Lily Thorne holding the cords. Frank Jolly left us in 1959 to become the rector of Thorpe St Andrew.

The Revd Jolly, 1952–59.

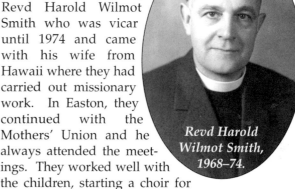

Above: *Mothers' Union festival service at the church, 1950s.*

Left: *The Revd Hugh Paine, 1959–68.*

Revd H.W. Paine served the church from 1959–66. Married with two step-children, he was a very quiet, kind and patient man. He died shortly after moving away from Easton.

He was followed by Revd Harold Wilmot Smith who was vicar until 1974 and came with his wife from Hawaii where they had carried out missionary work. In Easton, they continued with the Mothers' Union and he always attended the meetings. They worked well with the children, starting a choir for

Revd Harold Wilmot Smith, 1968–74.

both boys and girls who were taken back to the Vicarage after practice to make biscuits and sweets or small presents for Mum. The choir had no robes at this time, but mothers and friends made some for them. Revd Smith held a course of confirmation classes and in 1972 he took several young people to St Nicholas Church in Dereham to be confirmed.

Revd John Bliss *(left)* was vicar from 1974–80 and in just his second year at Easton found himself faced with the task of having to have the church roof renovated. The bell cote was removed, and new windows were fitted which left the parish with a bill for £8,000. Parishioners helped raise the money by selling

Right: *Rosemary Frost with the altar frontal which she made in the 1970s.*

Far right: *Mothers' Union banner carriers, 1950s. Left to right: Alice Sparkes, Doris Peacock and Lily Thorne.*

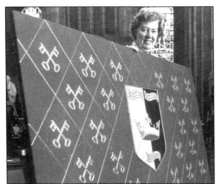

Left: *Confirmation at St Nicholas Church, Dereham, 1972. Left to right: Christine Ponder, Sandra Chapman, Vivienne Wiepen, Susan Wiepen, Cheryl Barker, Susan Cullum and Susan Simons.*

Below: *A group in the Old Vicarage with the Revd Bliss, 1970s.*

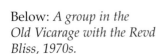

Above: *Easton Choir, 1980s. Left to right, back row: Paula Millwood, Alison Nesbit, Jillian Nelson, Adrian Gaskin, Andrew Pegg; middle row: Catherine Bunn, Kirstie Johnson, Simon Watson, Timothy Pease; front row: Kathryn Longbottom, Alison Pegg, Steven Pease.*

Left: *Mother and children all christened on the same day in September 1985. Pictured are Mum Sally and Dad Michael Wiepen, holding baby Simon. Children, left to right: Tina, Lyn and Claire.*

Below: Left to right: *Mrs Lily Scrutton, Revd Roger Burt, Mrs Ellen Gent, 1985.*

Above: *Mrs Barnard with hassocks of the cross keys, 1980s.*

Below: *Ladies and their hassocks, early 1980s. Left to right: Vera Barnard, Mrs Crowe, Joan Chapman, Doris Blogg, Doreen Green.*

home-made goods on the Hay Hill stall once a year. Another fund-raising venture, Revd Bliss' own brain-wave, started in 1977. Every Friday during the summer Mr Bill Sharp towed the 'Tea Caravan' to the lay-by near the church and set it up on the wide grass verge, beside the A47, whereupon Mrs Sharp and Mrs Blogg put the kettles on their little gas stove ready to make the teas to sell, with sandwiches and home-made cakes, to the holiday travellers. In those pioneering days of the caravan they slept in it and began very early, boiling the kettles for the Sunday-morning travellers. It wasn't long, however, before a rota system was organised and they no longer found it necessary to stay overnight. This rewarding venture continued well into the 1980s. It was very hard work and all the water had to be collected from the allotments opposite the church (at the time there was no kitchen in the church).

Although John had High Church persuasions, he was ecumenical and joined in village life to the full. The choir flourished under his leadership, he was on the Village Hall Committee, and helped run fêtes in the Vicarage garden and at Mr Rampton's. The elegantly furnished Vicarage was the scene of many a parish party following a festival service in the church where Daisy Sharp's meringues were a favourite, and it was John who started the Christingle Service, which is still an important date on the calendar for Christmas Eve. As Diocesan Furnishing Officer, he had the opportunity to search through redundant city churches and in the course of doing so found an ornate rood cross and pulpit for the church at Easton. His great companion was a dog which he had to give to a family in Wymondham when he moved to America.

Revd Roger Burt (below) was inducted to the living of Easton, Marlingford (added to the benefice during Revd Bliss' incumbency) and Colton on 28 July 1980. He had recently returned to England after nearly 14 years in New Zealand. Easton was not new to him, however, as he had been a student at the Agricultural College. During his time here he re-furnished the Lady chapel with new linen and renewed the altar frontals, also finding new cup-boards for storage. The new embroidered vestments were made in memory of Miss Rosetta Wilkinson who took up church embroidery when she retired from Norfolk and Norwich Hospital after working as a nurse for 50 years. The vestments were duly blessed. The Church Room was painted and repaired with almost totally new wire-mesh win-dows and gradually the hall began to be used by groups of parishioners once again.

In 1980 the Alternative Service Book was introduced. The statue of St Peter was reintroduced to the niche after being restored and blue votive lamps began to be used. The church bell, which had been stolen in the early 1970s, was replaced in August 1984 and installed by Mr Ireson and his son Robert of Easton. The date stone on the front wall of the porch was inscribed in 1985. Beginning in 1986 plans and fund-raising were in progress for a gallery spanning the church from the south door across the west end. This was finished in 1988 and is used for meetings, Sunday school and socials. Roger gathered together the young lads of the village and formed a task force for the improvement of the churchyards in the benefice, amongst other works. Many remember him riding round the parishes on horseback.

During 1989 Mr Fox of Easton converted the vestry into a kitchen and toilet. This was to provide a whole new dimension for the church, with a fitted sink unit, running water and a toilet/hand-washing facilities. It was completed by September. Porch doors were made and added to the south porch in 1990, having been bought using money given in memory of Noel Frost.

Revd Michael Allen (left) (1991–95), and his wife Sheila, were the first to live in the New Vicarage. By this time three parishes only war-ranted a half post, and his other job was as Diocesan Local Ministry Officer, encouraging the sharing of the traditional clergy role with lay people. When he found out about the Tea Caravan he called a meeting and in April 1991 the 'Easton Church Summer Project' was begun; after a great deal of preparation by a small committee and the wonderful help of many people in the village of Easton and beyond, the 'Church Café' opened its doors. The café opened every Saturday, provided there wasn't a wedding, from the end of May to the beginning of September.

Revd Jonathan Lumby (below) (1995–98) shared his parochial role with that of the Diocesan Rural Officer – and his donkeys and goats. The Diocesan Pilgrimage to St Walstan's Well, with donkeys and children, which he initiated, was a memorable event. Jonathan had a deep interest in things historical and the Map Exhibition held in Marlingford church was vis-ited by people from far and wide.

The new Diocesan House.
Below: *Harvest Festival in the church.*

In August 1993 the Old Vicarage was turned into the Diocesan Office, heralding a great loss to the community – this having been the venue for many events, including our annual fêtes, fireworks night parties, and more. There were many alterations made to both the inside and the outside of the building during its conversion.

Angela Reynolds became the vicar in March 1999. She was the first female priest for Easton and the surrounding parishes of Marlingford, Colton and Bawburgh, which was added in 2001. She has been married to Gordon for 34 years and lived for the first six years of marriage at Easton College (Norfolk School of Agriculture) where he was a lecturer. Gordon has been a great support to her in her change of role in later life. Angela was on the Parish Council and in the WI. Little did she think that she would be returning to the village as our vicar. She attends many village meetings, is involved in numerous organisations and is very busy with the school. She and Gordon have two daughters and two

grandchildren. Colin Hall, a relative newcomer to the village, penned these lines:

The Revd Angela is one of those clerics who never seems to have enough time to do anything for herself because she is always busy doing things for other people. She has, of course, a number of parishes to look after and Easton is but one. Nevertheless she gives freely of her time in supporting the school and all events and fund-raising in the village. She regards, quite rightly, that everyone in the community is part of her flock and she seeks to serve them whenever she is needed. She is a determined lady of very strong views and someone who is always prepared to genuinely listen and assist in whatever way she can. She has a great sense of humour and is at ease with people no matter what their so-called standing in life may be. It has been said that God has three sorts of servants in the world; some are slaves and serve Him from fear; others are hirelings and serve for wages; and the last are sons and daughters who serve because they love. Angela falls certainly into the latter as a priest who loves God and serves Him in love wherever she may be found.

The church, with its friendly congregation of community-minded individuals, is the centre of many activities and a very happy place to be.

Revd Angela Reynolds, 1999.

THE CHURCH OF OUR LADY AND ST PETER

YEAR		RECTORS
1310	-	Thomas de Depham
1317	-	Nicholas de Gosford
1349	-	William de Gosford
1359	-	Walter Urry of St Osith's
1364	-	Robert de Depedale
1370	-	Walter Yngald
1379	-	William Atte Fen

YEAR		VICARS
1403	-	William Reder
1403	-	Thomas Walsham
1412	-	John Bertelet
1414	-	John Balle
1414	-	John Bertelet
1417	-	Thomas Burgh
1420	-	John Forth
1438	-	Robert Primrose
1444	-	Richard Primrose
1452	-	John Chapman
1471	-	Edmund Agges (Aggys)
1486	-	Richard Vincent
1511	-	Richard Strete
1515	-	Thomas Kynsmen
1533	-	Thomas Carter
1555	-	Thomas Chevele
1560	-	George Mitchell
1585	-	George Mayhew
1594	-	Thomas Heache
1597	-	Francis Downes
1616	-	William Burgess
1619	-	John Reyner
16??	-	Christopher Stinnet
1663	-	Nicholas Barwick
1672	-	John Paris
1681	-	Bartholomew Harwood
1700	-	Thomas Patterson
1724	-	John Brand
1767	-	John Clement Ives
1783	-	Thomas Weatherhead
1809	-	John Fellowes
1836	-	Jonathan Chase Matchett
1873	-	James William Harding
1882	-	Warren James Blake
1914	-	W.E. Perrin
1928	-	B. Pugh
1932	-	Frank Bracecampe
1937	-	John Oswald Dean
1946	-	Harold Colwell-Smith
1952	-	Frank Jolly
1959	-	H. Paine
1968	-	Harold Wilmot Smith
1974	-	John Bliss
1980	-	Roger Burt
1988	-	No vicar
1991	-	Michael Allen
1995	-	Jonathan Lumby
1999	-	Angela Reynolds

Right: *A sketch of the north side of the church, early 1980s.*

Below: *The church when it had the screen, 1970s.*

Below right: *The church interior as it is at the time of writing.*

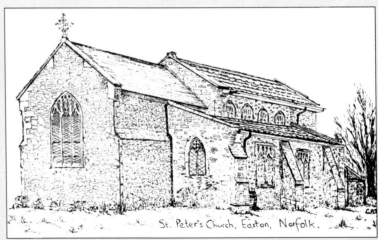

St. Peter's Church, Easton, Norfolk.

Chapter Three

Lower Easton

The History of Easton Lodge

The Lodge at Easton Heath commonly called Easton Lodge seems to be an ancient building and exceedingly strong, but I take it to be no more than designed for its present use, and was built to survey the Heath and resist the weather, which it stands much exposed to, it being formerly the Lodge of the Game-Keeper of 'Cossey Manor'.

So wrote Bloomfield in his eighteenth-century *History of Norfolk* (Vol. 11, p399). However, the belief that this building began life as a gamekeeper's lodge is questioned in the *History of the County of Norfolk* (Vol. 4, 1781). In fact, we cannot be sure exactly which building Bloomfield was referring to; Easton Lodge as we know it today is the seat of Leonard Buxton Esq., situated in a beautiful vale close to the water, and finely decorated with timber.

In 1832, some years after Bloomfield and his contemporaries made their claims, another Easton Lodge was built in Costessey Park, to the design of J.C. Bucker. This building was home to gardeners and gamekeepers employed by the estate up until 1918.

Bloomfield's assertion is not backed up by any existing records. The earliest document to refer to Easton Lodge, at Easton (known in the first half of the eighteenth century as Roods or Reeds House), is the will of John Norris, gentleman of Easton who was a maltster and a rural entrepreneur. He died in 1721. The Lodge (at that time in the occupation of John Bidewell), was left to John Norris' wife Susanna for the rest of her life – and to his son William he left his 'messuages, lands, tenements and herediments'. His other two children received £1,000 each. John Norris' estate was clearly substantial. Due to the absence of any earlier documents it would appear that he acquired the land of Easton Heath from the lord of the manor of Costessey, Sir Francis Jerningham, some time during the late-seventeenth or early-eighteenth centuries. He then proceeded to build himself a country seat of note.

English Heritage claim that Easton Lodge dates from the late-eighteenth century; this incorrect

Easton Lodge, 1779.

assumption seems to arise from the fact that a delightful illustration of the house was commissioned in 1779 *(below)*.

John Bidewell gave up his tenancy to Easton Lodge soon after the demise of John Norris. It seems that John Norris' son William moved in for we know that in 1725 William Norris moved out of Easton Lodge and offered it for rent. The next 25 years were difficult for him; records reveal little more about him other than the fact that he had become a 'chapman' (a trader or pedlar) as well as a maltster. On several occasions he was obliged to raise capital against Easton Lodge. The house was leased to various tenants, including Thomas Brimstone, yeoman, in the late 1720s and '30s, and Robert Rix in the 1740s.

In 1754 bankruptcy proceedings were brought against William Norris. His estate in Easton was put up for sale, and it was bought by Sarah Buxton for £1,700. Three years later, in 1757, she died; in the few years she had lived at Easton Lodge she had purchased further houses, tenements and land in Easton, to the value of £630. The estate passed to her brother, Leonard Buxton Esq., and bequests were made to her sister Ann Buxton (£30 per year), her nephew John Buxton (£1,000), and 'the poor of the Parish of Easton' (£5). Easton Lodge was Leonard Buxton's country seat for nearly 30 years, during which time he acquired hundreds of additional acres and other various properties in Easton through 'conveyances and exchanges'. Apart from these land purchases, Buxton also undertook a programme of building works at Easton Lodge. An illustration of the property, published in 1779, shows the improvements. Little if any attention had been lavished on the grounds surrounding the house. Leonard Buxton died in 1789 and he left everything to his nephew John Buxton.

During the late-eighteenth century the Easton estate had increased in size more than sevenfold from the 101 acres originally sold to Sarah Buxton in 1754. John Buxton, by this time the Revd John Buxton – rector of the Parish Church of Carleton Rode in Norfolk, where he also lived – had inherited a house he had no need of and an agricultural estate he had no desire to manage, and the following year, 1790, Easton estate was offered for sale. The buyer was Sir Lambert Blackwell, who paid 'a consideration of £5,000'.

Sir Lambert Blackwell (1732–1801) was a bachelor in the latter years of his life when he purchased Easton Lodge. He was the grandson of Sir Lambert Blackwell of Sprowston Hall, an MP, a gentleman of the Privy Chamber, and a member of the Diplomatic Service, who had been created a baronet by George I in 1718. The Sir Lambert Blackwell who moved to Easton Lodge in 1790 was the only son of Charles Blackwell and his wife Anne, daughter of Sir William Clayton.

Sir Lambert (1732–1801) was very fond of trees and planting, spending many hours in this peaceful pursuit, and he was responsible for introducing numerous different kinds of trees not found elsewhere in the area. Grigor, in his account of selected Norfolk residences, describes enthusiastically the grounds of

Easton Lodge as being 'highly romantic and amongst the loveliest scenes anywhere beheld' (1841). He writes:

The hall is pleasantly situated on a slope facing the south, commanding a plentiful woodland prospect and except in front is surrounded by a thick umbrageous screen, which shelters it even in winter. The great charm of this place is its choice collection of trees, deciduous and evergreen. As an arboretum, this place has an interest superior to any other spot in this county. Here we have specimens of all the leading ornamental trees suited to a British climate.

When Sir Lambert died the family title became extinct. The Easton Lodge estate was inherited by his kinsman, William Foster Esq., a solicitor of Norwich. He continued, leasing the farms, public house and lands of the estate, but kept Easton Lodge and gardens for his own use. In 1820 he died and his sons offered the house and estate for sale.

Left: *The lounge at Easton Lodge, late-nineteenth century.*

Right: *The drawing-room at Easton Lodge, late-nineteenth century.*

PARTICULARS OF A MOST COMPLETE AND DESIRABLE ESTATE
IN EASTON
IN THE COUNTY OF NORFOLK
A CAPITAL MESSUAGE CALLED
EASTON LODGE
To be sold by private contract

Most delightfully situated in a beautiful valley through which runs a fine stream of water and surrounded with hills clothed with fine oaks and large fir trees, with an excellent attached office, a double stable and coach-house, gardens, shrubberys, gardeners cottage, a farmhouse with barns and other buildings and 414 acres of arable, meadow, pasture, wood and Bruery land, late occupied by William Foster Esq. (deceased) the proprietor, and now in possession of his executives.

The capital messuage comprises on the ground floor, an Entrance hall, Dining room, a Drawing Room and Library, a spacious Kitchen and Offices.

A handsome messuage called West Lodge in the occupation of the Rev Frederick Bevan, 4 acres
A public house called The Dog in the occupation of Henry Balls, 9 acres
A farm in the occupation of Joseph Harman, 21 acres
A farmhouse in the occupation of William Clarke, 50 acres
A large cottage in the occupation of James Baxter, 5 acres
A good farmhouse in the occupation of Henry Balls 20 acres
12 good cottages

Arable 47 acres
Meadow or Pasture 150 acres
Wood 97 acres
Heath 54 acres
Roads 10 acres

Total 783 acres

Of the before mentioned Estate, 16 messuages, 2 tenements, 6 cottages, some small pieces of land, 8 parcels of Bruery and 389 acres of land are stated to be copy hold of the Manor of Costessey. The remainder of the estate is Freehold.

This beautiful estate, situated by the River Wensum, is in a ring fence and bounds with game and wildfowl. It would be difficult to find, even in these counties, the most picturesque scenery, a spot more richly adorned by all the beauties of nature, possessing every combination of hill and valley, wood and water. The roads about it in every direction are very good, and though completely sequestered, it is within seven miles of Norwich, forming in every respect a most complete and desirable residence for the man of taste and the sportsman.

The estate was sold to Thomas Trench Berney of Morton Hall for £31,500 – £19,500 for the freehold parts and £12,000 for the copyhold parts.

Thomas Trench Berney (1784–1869) was a JP and the High Sheriff of Norfolk in 1813 and was married to Mary Penrice. They had no intention of living at Easton Lodge themselves, which consisted of a mansion (Easton Lodge), a handsome messuage (West Lodge), a public house, a smithy and carpenter's shop, four farms, 14 cottages and a farmhouse, barn and stables in Cossey. It was bought as an investment and was leased in 1824 to a William Orton Salmon for eight years at a yearly rent of £109. Despite the income from Easton Lodge, Berney was short of funds. In 1825, he mortgaged the estates to William Salmon for £20,000. Interest was to be paid at £4 per year and, according to surviving correspondence, Thomas Berney frequently fell behind with his interest on this loan.

In May 1828 William Salmon died and his wife Elizabeth was to sublet the property from June 1829 until April 1831 to Mr Jerningham, a relation of the Earl of the manor of Costessey. In March 1833 Elizabeth came to live at the Lodge again and letters started going backwards and forwards between herself and Thomas Berney regarding the state of the gardens, pleasure grounds and house, the latter of which was in need of repairs. He pointed out that the repairs were her responsibility. In 1834 Mrs Salmon left Easton Lodge. Her dealings with Thomas Berney ended with a chancery suit in 1835, when the £20,000 loan was paid off.

Easton Lodge was unoccupied for two years and it was during this time that it underwent its important nineteenth-century additions.

In October 1836 Thomas Burney's niece, Miss Elizabeth Fountaine, her brother John and her sister Caroline took up residence at the newly extended and refurbished Easton Lodge.

Following their departure a new tenant was sought. This was to be John Henry Gurney, a descendant of the Norman baron of the same name, who had come to England with William in 1066. (Another of his descendants was John Gurney (1655–1721), a merchant of Norwich.) John Henry Gurney (1819–1890) was a young man in his late twenties, a member of the important banking family, who had recently married his cousin, Mary Gurney, ten years his junior. Easton Lodge was their first marital home. In 1849, three years after moving to Easton, John Henry Gurney signed a new eight-year lease with his landlord Thomas Trench Berney. In the

❧ Bugg & Kidd Families ❧

Left: Left to right: *Bessie, Malcolm, Mrs Bugg, Clarice and baby Glenis, c.1936.*

Above: *Hilda Bugg, Glenis Bugg and Harriet Reeve at Lower Easton, 1947.*

Right: *Wedding day of Clarice and Les Kidd in 1950 with parents George and Ivy Kidd (left) and Oliver and Hilda Bugg (right).*

Right: *Mr Oliver Bugg with prize-winning cow, Nati, in the early 1950s.*

Above: *Leslie and Clarice Kidd with children Richard and Valerie, 1960.*

census return for 1851, Gurney is reported as being a 'banker and farmer of 200 acres employing ten men and seven boys out of doors.' By 1851 he and Mary had a baby son, John Gurney junr, and had many staff to look after their needs in their employment.

John Gurney was an ambitious young man, who in 1854 was elected Member of Parliament for King's Lynn – a position he held for 11 years. The new appointment coincided with his decision to leave Easton Lodge and the family moved to Catton Hall, Norfolk. John later acquired an estate in Keswick.

By 1875, the Gurney family owned in excess of 11,500 acres in the county of Norfolk. John Henry Gurney died in 1890. His son became a JP, High Sheriff of Norfolk (1894) and was a Fellow of the Zoological and Linnean Society.

The remainder of Gurney's lease for Easton Lodge was taken over in 1854 by Henry Kelsall Esq., from Kochdale in Lancashire.

In 1859 Thomas Berney granted a new eight-year lease to John and Mary Ewart; John Ewart was a magistrate for the county of Leicestershire and a lieutenant in the Leicestershire Yeomanry (volunteer) Cavalry. Easton Lodge was a holiday home for the couple, infrequently used, and only the gardeners were in residence. By 1866 the Ewarts had given up the lease of Easton Lodge.

In 1869, Thomas Trench Berney died at Morton Hall, and was succeeded by his son George Duckett Berney. The tradition of leasing the Lodge continued and the next tenant was Frederick Garnett who was a captain with the 1st West Norfolk Militia and was married to Adeline with whom he fathered three sons; the couple employed seven live-in servants and remained at Easton Lodge for nearly 30 years.

In 1887 George Duckett Berney died and the ownership of Easton Lodge passed to his wife Catherine Mary Berney. A new tenant, Mrs Elizabeth Thorpe, took up residence and she remained until 1912. After her departure a new tenant, Mr Robert E. Parker, moved in, but by 1922 he had left Easton. George Berney and his mother died and the trustees of the estate decided to offer Easton Lodge for sale.

In August 1923, the Easton Lodge estate was sold to Mr Colin Kidner who, as well as farming, was very active in village affairs – notably serving as secretary to the Village Hall committee. Together with the committee's chairman, Mr George Jennings, he had a tenancy agreement with Bullard & Sons who owned the hall (which stood next to The Dog).

One of the many employed by Colin Kidner was Oliver Bugg who moved from Braconash with his wife Hilda and their five children – Bessie, Clarice, Malcolm, Glenis and Ivor – into a tied cottage on Easton Lodge estate where Oliver worked as a cowman for several years. On leaving school, Clarice worked for seven years for Mrs Kidner in the house on the domestic side and was also nanny to the grandchildren. After Mr Colin Kidner sold Easton Lodge

estate he went to Colton Fruit Farm. Col Forbes came to live at Easton Lodge estate in the late 1940s and Clarice continued to work for them for a time. She met Leslie Kidd who lived with his parents George and Ivy Kidd at the Negro's Head public house at Colton and they were married in 1950 at Easton church and had their reception in the Church Room (known as the Green Hut). Then they moved to Sundial Cottage at Colton. Leslie was a lorry driver for the Colton estates and they lived in Colton for 17 years before moving back to Easton in 1968. They have a daughter Valerie, a son Richard and four grandsons.

Mr J. Rampton and his family came to Easton Lodge in 1963 and since that time has been very good to the village, allowing fêtes to be held on their land and the Village Hall committee to stage a yearly barbecue, dancing on the tennis-courts and swimming in the pool.

Listed below are some of his many workers and their families who have worked for him on the estate:

Jim Davison (and Family)	Gardener
Jim Butler	Farm manager
Bernard Frost	Farm manager
R. Nurse	Tractor driver
Jack Stapleton (and Family)	Mechanic
Freddie Anderson	Woodman
Jack Lawson	Pig man
John Sallis	Farm manager
Colin Mattless (and Family)	Cowman (29 years)
Lennie Bayfield (1965–c.'86)	Gamekeeper
Peter Frost (and Family)	Tractor driver and pig man all his working life

A map in the Norwich Museum shows that in 1849 a hoard of silver was found in a field on the right going down Dog Hill, which leads to Easton Lodge estate.

At the junction of Church Lane and Ringland Lane was The Cross (below) – otherwise known as 'The Stump' – which stood on a green mound and was of flint and mortar similar to the remains of the church tower. The full facts have never been discovered, but it is thought that this was a meeting-place for pilgrims.

Left: *The Kitchen Garden Cottage on the Easton estate, c.1970s.*

Below: *Molly and Colin Mattless and family at Riverside Cottage, c.1971.*

Above: *Lennie Bayfield, c.1980s.*

Right: *Matthew Rampton presenting Mr Lennie Bayfield, gamekeeper, with a picture of Easton Lodge estate on his retirement.*

Right and far right: *The drive at Easton Lodge White Gates, late 1980s.*

Right: *The drive at Easton Lodge, late 1980s.*

Poultry farm, Easton Lodge, 1937.

Easton Poultry Farm and Egg-Packing Station

Situated at Lower Easton on the Easton estate on higher ground behind Easton Lodge and the dairy owned by Mr Colin Kidner, the poultry farm and egg-packing station was quite a thriving business, providing employment for several men and women. The manager was Mr Meredith. Second from the left in the photograph shown above is Bert Wright from Honingham who started work there in 1937. Arthur Haines is the man holding the lorry door. The second man from the left in the group by the Model-T Ford is William (Billy) Hanwell from Honingham who cycled from Honingham to Easton twice daily to look after the incubators. Other people who worked on the site included Donald Greenacre from Easton, Tom Wright from Honingham, Cyril Clark from Honingham, Mrs Evelyn Greenacre, Miss Daisy Mobbs and Roland (Tottie) Chapman from Easton. The poultry farm moved from Easton to Bawburgh c.1950.

Evelyn Blyth (née Spooner, born 1927)

My memories of Easton are from when I was four-and-a-half years old and moving to Lodge Farm Cottages, from Bickerstone near Colton (where I was born) with my parents and sister. We walked nearly two miles to school each day, where we were very happy and enjoyed our years there until we left at 14 years old, having gained many friends. We progressed from what was called the 'little room' with our teacher Miss Seaman to the 'big room' where Miss Taylor taught us with great expertise.

Other lovely memories are of the nativity plays in the church and dancing round the Maypole on the green to an old gramophone near the old St Peter's Church Room opposite the church, and fêtes in the Vicarage grounds with fancy-dress competitions which proved successful for my sister and I as the 'Bisto Kids'. Sledging down the Dog and Grass Hill was much enjoyed in winter, as also was spinning-tops and hopscotch when we could find a rare piece of tarred road.

Our holidays on the farm were idyllic, especially at harvest time, and I would get up early to accompany my Dad on his milk round to the surrounding villages where he would ladle the milk from the churn into jugs on the doorsteps. My mother would await his return to clean all the utensils and dairy equipment, meanwhile churning and making butter for the 'big house' across the road where the boss Colin Kidner lived.

My halcyon days of childhood were shattered at the outbreak of the Second World War and at the awful wail of the siren. We were ushered to the big reinforced cellar of the Kidner's house where all the farm workers were invited to assemble. Our house was equipped with an extension bell alerting all cottages on the farm and a rota was formed for a 'duty man' every night. At the all-clear we would often walk back at dawn – it was all misty and too cold to try to sleep. Never to be forgotten was the first night Norwich was bombed, in April 1942. My sister and friends, by then all teenagers, were at a dance in Bawburgh and we were transported home in an Army lorry (bikes and all) by the REME soldiers stationed at Model Farm, Easton. The sight of the lit-up sky and the way the ground was lit up by lights dropped by the bombers to enable them to see their targets was terrifying as we travelled home to our parents frantically waiting at the White Gates.

Another poignant memory is of the untimely and tragic death in the Far East of our wonderful vicar, John O. Dean, who had volunteered for active service.

In spite of all this, many socials and dances were being held in Tucks Barn and the Church Room where we would dance with the solders from Model Farm. The Americans stationed at Weston Airfield

Above: *Dian Roberson* (on bike) *and Maureen Harrowven, c.1947.*

Below: *Dian Roberson and Peter Frost, Easton Lodge estate c.1956.*

Above: *Dian Roberson with Penny, c.1948.*

Left: *Dian Roberson, c.1955, during her time working as a dairymaid for the Easton Lodge estate, at the Royal Norfolk Show, Costessey. Countess the cow won the 'Supreme Championship'.*

Below: *The Queen presenting Peter Frost with a long-service award on 25 June 1986. He had served for 41 years at Easton Lodge estate.*

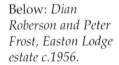

Mr Billy Spooner and Edie with (front) Evelyn, Daphne and baby John, 1941.

Memories of Dian Frost (née Roberson)

I was born on 29 September 1939, National Registration Day. Life down in Lower Easton was a bit tough – no electricity or water and a lav across the yard, but in one way they were the richest days of my life. Fred and Harriett were my grandparents and Nanny and Grandad Roberson just down the road were all there to help bring me up. I lived on dried milk and cod-liver oil, orange juice from Mr Loseby, a slice of bacon from the pig Grandad had cured and hung in the dairy and lots of full-cream milk from the Jersey cows which lived in the stable, and plenty of rabbit pie, roast pheasant or hare for which Grandad went poaching.

When the war was over Dad came home and we lodged in Norwich as there was no room at the Thatched House (Bellvue). I got a place at the Notre Dame [school], but I hated living in Norwich and soon became ill. The doctor was called and he thought it best if I went back to the country. I had to catch the bus into Norwich for school every day, and I was scared of walking up and down the hill (Dog Lane).

School-days were soon over and I had to get a job. Well, Grandad got me one down at Easton Lodge as a dairymaid for about 50 milking Ayrshires which belonged to Col Forbes. My day started about five in the morning getting the cows up. They all had names, and knew just what to do (more than I did); I used to wash the udders then the tails and then strip milk to make sure there was no mastitis.

I had only been there a few weeks when I made up my mind I was going to marry the foreman (Mother nearly had a fit). Well, that happened on 1 November 1958 and we lived at Thwaites Cottage with all modern conveniences and then it was not long before the children came along. Col Forbes then decided to sell Easton Lodge which was bought by Mr and Mrs Rampton in June 1963.

I still worked a few hours for him helping to raise the beef calves. The farm got bigger and we moved to Hill Farm; it was like living in a palace, a walk-in cloakroom with a shower, no more smelly boots and coats drying round the fire. We were able to keep a horse in the stable and graze it in the paddock. The children also had ducks and chickens – one of the chickens always laid her eggs under the sink in the cloakroom.

Life was very good and most of the time peaceful. Our early upbringing at St Peter's had a big influence on our lives. We still lead a good life and my husband Peter still works for Easton Lodge estate during the shooting season.

Evelyn and Heddy Blyth's wedding, 1947.

provided us with lavish parties in the hall with goodies that were otherwise unobtainable to us.

During the war we had an evacuee girl of 14 who came in 1941 and stayed with us for nearly a year; we are still great friends. We keep in touch to this day telling her all the family news. We cycled to dances at Weston held in the hangars there and enjoyed top-class bands. When thankfully the war ended in 1945 I was planning my wedding and in November 1947 I was married at Easton church, so altogether I have very pleasant memories of the village of Easton.

Dian and Peter Frost, c.1990s.

🌿 The Thatched House 🌿

Tottie Ottaway (née Harrowven) was born at the Thatched House (Bellvue) where she lived with her nine brothers and sisters and where her father Fred worked on the land and kept cattle. The house is very much the same as it was then, with small windows, two rooms up and two rooms down. A slaughterhouse and small dairy were added to the house.

At the time of writing, Tottie is 92 years old and still lives in the house, which is the oldest dwelling in the village. She recalls seven incendiary bombs being dropped causing damage to the house during the Second World War. The whole family had to live in a chicken house until repairs were made. A Land Army girl during the war, Tottie married Ben Ottaway but had no children.

Left: *Fred and Harriet (Tottie's parents) with family in the early 1900s.*

Right: *Tottie in her Land Army uniform, 1940s.*

Left: *The Thatched House (Bellvue) at Lower Easton, which dates back to 1728.*

Right: *Harriet at the Thatched House (Bellvue), 1928.*

Far right: *Ben and Tottie Ottaway, 1989.*

John and Violet King

John King was born in Easton in 1925 and was the son of Alfred King, and the youngest of seven children. He went to Easton School and passed the 11-plus examination and then went to the City of Norwich School. After leaving school John had several jobs before he was called up into the REME and

John King, 1945.

was stationed at Leiston where he met Violet, who was born at Friston, Saxmundham. He spent a lot of his time in India, and when he was demobbed he came back to live with his father at Easton. In 1951 John and Violet were married at Easton church and they lived in one of the three cottages down by the ford. He worked at Hill Farm, farmed by Mr Wales, as a cowman for a time, then worked at the Woodworkers and was promoted to foreman and remained there until it closed down in the early 1990s.

He was a strong British Legion man and was a Freeman of the City of Norwich, an honour handed down to him from his father. He was a keen bowls player and bowled for Colton and Easton.

John and Violet have a son, Andrew, who has played bowls for Norfolk, and two grandchildren. John was always ready to help anyone, whoever it was, and you would see him, with his hat on, riding his bicycle about the village – he was a real character.

Left: *Billy Flowers and John King, 1930s.*

Violet and John King and grandchildren.

Phyllis Singleton (née Kidd)

In the wintertime we were often snowed in for about four to six weeks at a time and the roadmen had to cut a track to us as the snow was very deep and we had a job to walk. My Dad and I helped to pull cars out of the River Tud and clean out the mud as the river was very strong and deep. I can remember once when a car got stuck under the footbridge, the couple had to get out of the car and stand on the roof and we helped them onto the bridge to safety. The road men swept the concrete as the river made it very slippery. In January 1968 a road bridge was installed over the ford and this made it a lot easier for everyone.

I have lived here all my life in the same cottage by the river; it was lovely in the summer, picnics by the river and fishing with jamjars. My Dad caught fish out of the river at night by tickling their tummies, and my sister Ann was often with him.

I did have a smallholding with goats, chickens and a Shetland pony, but nowadays I just have a dog and keep chickens.

Above: *The ford at Lower Easton before the bridge was built.*

Below: *The bridge was built in 1968.*

❧ Ford at ❧
Lower Easton

Clockwise from left:
*The ford at Easton during the
1960s; date unknown; in
the 1890s; and in the 1950s.*

Easton School juniors
(above) *and seniors* **(this picture)***, 1945.*

The Stevensons

Sarah and Isaac Harry Stevenson came to Lower Easton when they were married to live in one of the three cottages near the River Tud. The two other cottages were occupied by Annie and Herbert Kidd and Violet and John King. Sarah worked at the college as a cook and Isaac was an insurance man. They had two children, Pat and Margaret, who both went to Easton School, and Pat remembers in 1945 all the children at school receiving a Red Cross parcel with soap, toothbrushes, etc. in them. Pat married Brian Leonard at Easton church then they moved away, but later on they came back to Easton to live.

Farming Days at West Lodge Farm

by Heriot John Cossey

My father Ken Cossey farmed at West Lodge Farm from 1934–68 with approximately 60 acres of arable land. I was born in 1937 and my younger sister Gillian in 1944. Father also kept bullocks in the yard during the wintertime to fatten, and these were sold at Norwich Market during early spring. In the early days he ploughed with horses, Captain and Major, which were stabled at West Lodge Farm. The water from the River Tud was brought up the road in a cart for the horses. As I grew up I helped my father on the farm; in the winter it was grinding by hand – mangels, swedes and chaff. In the summer months my school friend Ivor Bugg often helped with hoeing the sugar beet. Harvest was very hard as everything had to be done by hand, which involved long hours in the field until dark. Corn was brought down Church Lane to the stack-yard ready to be threshed in the winter. I remember the threshing being done by Fred Dann from North Tuddenham – early on it was done by steam engine and later on by tractor. We also kept chickens and sold the eggs to Easton Egg-Packing Station, at Easton Lodge.

My father was known locally as a 'poacher'; if a pheasant crossed his path, nine times out of ten it would be his. My father was a bowls player and played for Norfolk, and in his earlier days he played cricket; he was a real Norfolk countryman, a familiar figure walking the lanes with his dog.

Royalists and Parliamentarians at Lower Easton on 2 September 1984, in a re-enactment of events which took place c.1650. The Royalists, led by Revd Burt, proceeded along Church Lane to the Heath and were met by the Parliamentarians, organised by Mr Peter Williams (Sealed Knot Society). Finally the Royalist forces succumbed in ambush!

🌿 West Lodge Farm 🌿

Left: Left to right: *Grandad Cossey, Ken, Great-Granny Grey, baby Heriot, 1937.*

Below: *Heriot a little older, with his sister Gillian, c.1948.*

Far left: *Neil Baxter and Christopher Cossey playing in the snow at West Lodge Farm, c.1980s.*

Left: *Karin, a visitor to the area, in the stack-yard at West Lodge Farm, c.1965.*

Chapter Four

Families, Characters & Memories

Alfred King

Alfred and Sarah King and family moved to Easton – and into the house previously owned by a Mr Dallas – in 1912, having come from Edgefield, near Holt, where Alfred had made the churchyard gates. He was a blacksmith, farrier and wheelwright, and shod horses for the farmers in and around Easton, also making the wooden cartwheels (a task rarely carried out in those days by a regular carpenter). He then put the iron rims on them at the back of the house where there was a circular iron platform with a hole in the centre for the hub of the wheel. Alfred was also an engineer, and sold petrol, white spirit and paraffin. The petrol and white spirit was sold in two-gallon cans in the days before hand petrol pumps had been fitted (which in turn were later replaced by electrically-run pumps). When the pumps were installed Alfred also sold motor oil which was kept in cabinets between the petrol pumps. One of his many other jobs was sharpening shears and blades for lawnmowers.

As if he did not have enough to do, Alfred also ran a taxi service in the early 1930s and was one of the few people in Easton to own his own car (others being Charlie Hart and the Revd Dean).

At one time Alfred was also the only person in Easton to have a telephone. This did him no favours, however, as the machine was in demand at all hours, day and night, and he had it removed, arranging instead for one to be installed on the car park of the pub which at that time was run by people named Bridges.

Mrs Sarah King ran the shop, only one of two in the village, stocking just about everything anyone could want, and she would obtain other items for people if they were not in stock. Towards the end of the war crisps were added to the range of goods, as also was ice-cream (at that time called 'oky cokey') made by Pat Macs. The shop also stocked Norfolk Champion boots – a high-quality and expensive form of footwear with an excellent reputation. The farm labourers used to be paid a bonus and came to the shop to buy these boots when they received their money. Lovely vines covered the walls of the shop and children on their way home from school were often presented by Mr King with a handful of juicy black grapes. Alfred was made a Freeman of the City of Norwich on 30 June 1933.

When the couple moved to Easton, they had two children, Alfred and Olive, then later Ethel, Muriel, Bernard, Harry and John were born. The midwife came from Bawburgh and her name was Nurse Young. Muriel became a missionary in Brazil, where she is still living aged 86 at the time of writing!

Easton was a very small village at the time the King family moved there, and the nightingales used to sing in the woods near where the showground is now situated. The pub landlord owned the fields at the back of the shop. The family cats used to go over there and bring back rabbits. The grounds of their house were fairly extensive and included a large orchard with many fruit trees. Originally there was no running water, and the toilet was housed in a castellated building a few yards up, opposite the back door. The Kings' granddaughter still remembers the toilet paper as being the tissue wrappings from oranges. This was better than newspaper, which lots of other people had to use, and which was always threaded on string and hanging from a hook.

Mr and Mrs King retired in October 1959 and moved back to Lakenham where they had both been born and raised.

Alfred and Sarah King, 1966.

Bernard 'Bunny' (left) and Harry (right) King, 1943.

🌹 **Kings** 🌹

Left: *A King family outing to Great Yarmouth, 1927.*

Below left: *Joy and her grandfather, Mr King, holding the black grapes which grew on the shop wall, 1950.*

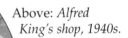

Above: *Alfred King's shop, 1940s.*

Left: *Mr Robert Scarfe (left) and Alfred King outside the shop in the 1940s.*

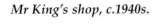

Mr King's shop, c.1940s.

The Chapman Family
by Joan Chapman

Tom and Blanche Chapman moved to Easton from Costessey Hall in 1913. He became the gamekeeper to Lee Smiths who owned Easton Hall at that time. The couple lived in Keepers Cottage on Hall Road for several years. They had five children: Raymond, Roland, Royston, Blanche and Ronald (who was born in Keepers Cottage in 1920).

Tom lost his right arm at Salonica during the First World War and the couple then moved to a house on the corner of Dereham and Marlingford Roads where they had a shop in the front room for a time in the early 1920s as Tom was unable to work. After a while he began doing odd gardening jobs; he worked at the Vicarage and for Ernest Morse the rose grower, who lived in Costessey Lodge. The Chapmans moved once again in 1934 – this time up to the new council-houses which boasted pail toilets in the back gardens. All the water had to be pumped up, but the family were lucky as the pump was more or less in their front garden. (The other village pump was at the pub.)

Tom resumed his work as a gamekeeper and was employed at Honingham Hall for several years. He was there when Sir Eric Tiechman was shot and killed by an American serviceman during the Second World War. He rode a 'sit-up-and-beg' bike with a fixed wheel brake and carried his bag and gun on his back. He played bowls down at the Church Room for Easton and is pictured in an old photograph of the bowls team.

Blanche used to enjoy a game of whist in the Church Room or with friends in the nearby villages, to which she would travel by bicycle.

Royston died of diphtheria in his third year. Blanche died in 1963 aged 72 and Tom died in 1968 aged 87 – both are buried in Easton churchyard.

I married Ronald in 1948. We have four children, ten grandchildren, and one great-grandchild. There are still Chapmans in the village at the time of writing. For 38 years of our married life Ronald and I lived in the Airey Houses on Marlingford Road, but I now live in Parkers Close.

Clockwise from above: *Tom Chapman, early 1900s; Tom Chapman, 1914; Tom Chapman in the Vicarage garden with Shot the dog, 1920s; Ronald Chapman, 1922; Ronald Chapman aged 14 years.*

Ronald and Joan Chapman
on their wedding day,
January 1948.

Chapmans

Left: *Ronald Chapman
outside the council-
houses in 1934.*

Below: *The Chapmans'
home at the Airey Houses,
1970s.*

Below left: *Receipt for
a Raleigh bike.*

Bottom right: *Ronald and
Joan Chapman on the day
of their ruby wedding,
January 1988.*

Below: *The Chapman
family. Left to right:
Tottie (Roland), Dinkie
(Blanche), Ena and
Ronnie (Ronald), 1980s.*

Ellen and Archie Gent

Ellen and Archie Gent moved from Colton to Easton in 1936 to a new bungalow on the Dereham Road. This had a bathroom and a flush toilet – a true luxury in those days for anyone who had come from a two-up, two-down cottage with a toilet way down the garden. There were three children: Edward (Ted), Joan and Pat.

In 1937 Gran Maria and Grandad Billy Smith moved from Colton to live with the family, as Maria was bedridden and needed care. Sadly she died shortly after, but Billy continued to live at the bungalow until his death on 11 December 1949, aged 89.

Archie worked for R.G. Carter of Drayton as a painter and decorator journeyman and the only means of transport available was a bicycle. During the war he was attached to the RAF and posted to St Athens in South Wales. Archie returned home from Wales in October 1945 and went back to work for R.G. Carter. He died suddenly on what was to turn out to be the same date as his father-in-law's death – 11 December – in 1945, aged just 51. It was only six weeks since he had returned home.

Ellen and Archie Gent, 1919.

Ellen worked for the NAAFI at Model Farm in Easton and then went to Bussy and Sabberton in Palace Street, Norwich, as a motor mechanic, repairing Army vehicles, which she also learned to drive. After the conflict she was employed at Trevor Page's in Norwich and was trained to make curtains and upholstery. She did this for a couple of years, then moved to London and worked as a live-in cook and housekeeper for a Harley Street doctor. This she did until able to afford her own flat. Ellen stayed in London for many years working as a cook in several big houses. She was with Lady and Sir Charles Dodds for about ten years. She also did upholstery and curtain making from home in her spare time. She did a lot of sewing for celebrities and for royalty, never charging enough for her services. She had a heart attack in 1972 and was fitted with a pacemaker at the Brompton Hospital. She came home to Easton and lived with Pat until being allocated a council bungalow in a sheltered-housing complex at Hethersett, where she lived for 18 years. During this period she was a member of Easton Good Companions Club. Her greatest joy was to travel and

nowhere was too far for her. She even went to Tenerife for her 90th birthday. Sadly she died four weeks before her 92nd birthday. She is buried with Archie in Easton churchyard.

Their son Ted passed a scholarship at Honingham School in 1935, took up a naval scholarship at the age of 13 and went to the training ship *Mercury* at Hamble in Hampshire, returning home for short visits only. Throughout the war years he served on HMS *Nelson* and in the mid-1950s supervised bringing mine-sweepers into Lowestoft Dockyard for repairs and trials. He served in the Navy for 40 years and was then employed in Royal Naval recruitment. He lived with his family in Edinburgh, but liked to spend as much time as possible here in Easton. He passed away in December 2001 at the age of 79.

Joan's first employers were Mr and Mrs Hyde-Clarke who had spent many years working in Darjeeling in India as tea planters. They came to live in the woods on the boundary between Easton and Costessey (opposite the showground). In their grounds they had a very large area of double-wired enclosures and runs, in which they kept silver foxes which were bred for their pelts. Leaving the employment of the Hyde-Clarkes, Joan worked at Howes Garage in Chapelfield, Norwich, as an airframe fitter on Sterling Aircraft. From there she went to Caley's Chocolate Factory, which was taken over to make batteries for tanks. Then she moved on to Howlet & Whites making shoes. She was still living at home when she met and married Ronnie Chapman in 1948. They moved into a new Airey House on Marlingford Road in 1949. At the time of writing, Joan lives in a bungalow in Parkers Close, Easton.

Pat joined the Land Army and went to work for a Mr Chamberlain at Hall Farm, Easton. This was shortly before it became the School of Agriculture. She continued working on the land for around 40 years, doing all sorts of jobs. The one she most hated was threshing a corn stack and having rats running round her legs. Later on it was more vegetables, hoeing sugar beet, picking up tons of potatoes by hand and trimming tons of Brussels sprouts by hand. These were happy times, although it didn't seem so at the time. Pat married Theo Wiepen in 1947 and they still live in the same bungalow in the village in 2004.

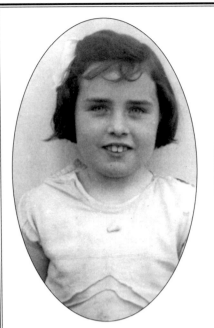

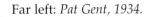

Far left: *Pat Gent, 1934.*

Left: *Joan Gent, 1934.*

Below: *William Smith and an American soldier friend, 1940s.*

Below centre: *Archie and Ellen, and Pat and Joan Gent, 1932.*

Below left: *William and Maria Smith, the parents of Ellen Gent, 1930.*

A trip to the seaside, 1924. Left to right, back row: *? Tripp, Archie Gent, Ellen Gent, Maria Smith, Edith Howard;* front row: *Ted Gent, Rosie Smith.*

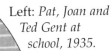

Left: *Pat, Joan and Ted Gent at school, 1935.*

Below left: *The 90th birthday of Ellen Gent in June 1990.* Left to right: *Joan, Ellen, Pat.*

Gents

Left: *Mother and son, Ellen and Ted Gent, 1950s.*

Left: Left to right: *Joan, Pat and Ellen Gent, 1940s.*

Right: *Archie Gent, 1944.*

Below right: Left to right: *Joan Chapman and Pat Wiepen (sisters), 1998.*

Left: *Ted Gent, 1934.*

Below: *The Gent family, 1990s.* Left to right: *Pat, Ted and Joan.*

Freddie Fox junr

We came to Easton as evacuees from Lowestoft in 1941 to get away from the heavy bombing. I was just 12 years old. We moved into a cottage in a small yard near Rose Cottages, next door to my dad's sister, Mary Shingles. I remember the times when they drove the cattle and sheep from Norwich Market through the village on Saturday afternoons. If a gate was left open everything would be smashed up. I left school at 14 and got a job at Bally and Holstine shoe factory. At this time my Dad, Fred, worked on the airfield at Attlebridge. When he got called up into the Army my Mother and I returned to Lowestoft. I got work at Brooke Marine Shipyard as an apprentice electric welder, which I did for two years. When Dad was demobbed I broke my trade and went to work with him in the fish houses, preparing the herring for the smokehouse, to emerge as kippers.

We came back to live in Easton in 1946, as my parents had bought my grandfather's bungalow on Dereham Road. Dad worked for a time at Hall Farm for Mr Chamberlain and then with Norfolk County Council as a lengthman on the roads for 24 years. He was a very well-known person who took pride in his work; the verges were always straight and tidy and all potholes were filled as he went along. When we had snow, which we did have a lot of in those days, he would help Kenny Cossey with the sanding of the roads and using the snowplough. I got work at the woodworker's in the village. Jimmy Ponder was foreman at that time, and then worked at Hall Farm helping Fred Parsons with the cows and bottling milk ready for early-morning collection and delivery. Mum, 'Dolly', was employed as a domestic help at the Dr Barnardo's Home at Honingham Hall for several years. It was a long drag to cycle there and back every day. From there she then went to the School of Agriculture and then by bus into Norwich each day to Princes Restaurant on Guildhall Hill. Mum worked until she was 73 years old.

When still at school I used to bike down to the butcher's shop at Bawburgh, and this is where I first met Doris. She would sometimes be collecting meat for her mother. We got to be good friends. We met up again when I was 18 and got married at 19 years of age. We moved into a cottage on Bawburgh Road in 1948 and are still living there 55 years later. We have one daughter and one granddaughter.

There were no other houses in the road at that time, only Bob Bucks' shop on the corner. We have seen many council-houses and bungalows built on the left-hand side, about 50 in all. There is now a new housing estate taking shape on the right-hand side. There have been a lot of changes since I came to Easton in 1941.

My Dad Fred died aged 75 and Mum died two years later. Both are buried in Lowestoft.

Left: *Dolly and Freddie Fox senr with Freddie junr, 1940s.*

Below: *Dolly Fox, 1940s.*

Right: *Freddie Fox senr, 1970s.*

Right: *Fred Fox senr and great-granddaughter Carolyn looking down to the river at Lower Easton, 1951.*

Below: *Doris and Freddie junr, 1959.*

Left: *Freddie junr in 1981.*

Far right: *Doris and Freddie junr, 1950.*

Left: *George (a fishmonger) and Emma Harrowven, 1890s.*

The Harrowven Family

by Robert Harrowven, born 26 November 1929

My great-grandfather, Tom Harrowven, was born at Easton in the middle of the nineteenth century. He was a gamekeeper. He married Jane and they raised ten children. Fred Harrowven was one of the children and lived in the Thatched House in Lower Easton (Bellvue), the oldest house in the village. [His story appears later in this book.]

My grandfather, George, also one of the ten children, lived up in the village opposite The Dog pub. His wife was called was Emma and they had five children, four daughters and one son (my father Sidney). George ran a pony and cart selling fish around the neighbouring villages and he smoked his own kippers in a small shed at the back of the cottage. He would go up to St Benedicts in Norwich to buy the fish early in the morning and I would often go with him to Marlingford to have the pony shod by the blacksmith there.

My father joined the Navy at the age of 16, during the First World War, and when he came out he married my mother Daisy. With the money he came out with, £70, he bought a piece of land along the main road and built his own bungalow, as well as greenhouses and sheds; he grew salad crops, kept pigs and worked on the land around the bungalow. I had five brothers and three sisters.

Before she got married my mother had been in service, and later she also helped my father on the land. After school we were expected to help with the work – especially the older ones. My father was a very industrious man and my brothers and I have had a lot of his skills passed down to us, including carpentry, building, etc. He worked in the building trade and during the Second World War he cycled back to the city at night to fire-watch the schools.

I have always lived in the village and worked on the land. I also worked for Lawrence & Scott for 33 years as a machinist. I retired in 1993. My wife, Hazel, has one daughter (my stepdaughter) and two grandchildren. Easton is home to me and although it has changed a great deal I still remember how it was. Lower Easton and the river are much the same as they were when I was a boy.

Tom Harrowven, late 1800s.

Right: *Daisy Harrowven, 1920s.*

Below: *Maud, Bea and Sidney, early 1900s.*

❦ *Harrowvens* ❦

Above: *Sidney and Daisy Harrowven, 1950s.*

Right: *Sidney Harrowven, 1920s.*

Far right: *Eva and Edna Harrowven, early 1900s.*

Below: *Robert (son of Sidney and Daisy) and Hazel Harrowven, 2000.*

Above far right: *Robert Harrowven aged 20, 1949.*

Right: *Daisy and Sidney Harrowven's house which was built in the 1920s.*

Jack and Emily Hurrell

In the early 1920s, after serving in the Army during the First World War, Jack *(left, c.1914–18)* and Emily Hurrell *(below, 1940s)* came to live in Easton. They lived in a cottage near the Old School and Jack bought a field adjoining the cottage, which was the start of a lot of hard work for them both. The field had to be cleared of many trees before they were able to buy and bring home a railway carriage to live in, thus leaving the cottage. They lived there for approximately 30 years. It was quite spacious, with a large living-room and two bedrooms; a kitchen was added later. The couple had two sons and a daughter.

The land was turned into a very good smallholding with a horse helping with the heavier work. Jack provided the village with fruit and vegetables of all descriptions for many years after the addition of a large greenhouse. Here they grew the best-flavoured tomatoes ever tasted.

During the summer months when his water tanks ran low Jack would take the horse and cart and a tank down Dog Hill to the River Tud. He filled the tank with water but, coming back, the weight of the water was too much for the horse to pull up the hill so they would come back along Church Lane and on to the turnpike (Dereham Road). Drinking-water had to be fetched and carried in a pail from the pump near The Dog.

For many years Emily and Jack went to Norwich every Friday morning with the horse and cart laden with fruit, eggs and vegetables, which they sold to many regular customers who would be waiting for them along the Dereham Road on the way into Norwich. Later Jack hired the glebe fields around the church which he cropped with corn and sugar beet. He also took on another glebe field opposite the church, which had the Church Room in the corner and bowling-green adjoining. The biggest part of the field was the football pitch – before he took it over that is; in 2004 this area is the village allotments. With just a horse to plough and drill it was hard work and involved long hours tramping many miles a day.

Alfred King had buildings on the turnpike near The Dog from where he ran a forge in which he shod the horses for Jack, but after he closed up the nearest forge was quite a walk away. In 1935 Jack was in charge of the old Village Hall, which adjoined

buildings that belonged to The Dog. In 1939 he ran the Howes Charity for the poor of the village and was also on various school and village committees. (He was also a school manager.) Another regular job he did was emptying the pails in the school toilets; some sources believe this was called 'scavaging'.

During the Second World War the two boys went into the Army; Basil, the youngest son, was killed in action in Italy, and was buried in Cassino Memorial Cemetery, Italy, in 1944 at the age of 23.

Around 1950 a small tractor made a great difference to getting the work done. Jack and Emily's daughter Lily drove the tractor for harrowing and rolling which gave Jack more time for the smaller jobs which he carried out, still using the horse. On Sundays Jack became the village hairdresser and had many customers, men, boys and girls. A good haircut cost one shilling. Bertie Sparkes said that as a boy Mr Hurrell put a pudding basin on his head and cut around it. Jack really was a 'Jack of all Trades'!

In 1953 the couple had a bungalow built where they enjoyed around 20 years of easier living, which they well deserved. This was the first bungalow to be built on what is now the Woodview estate. Grady Builders bought the land in around 1960 and a few houses were built on the right-hand side of the Loke (farm track). The Jubilee Playing Field, given to the village by Mr Lee Smith, is on the left. Jack died in 1974 and Emily 1975.

Above: *Jack examining a piece of Zeppelin in a field at Easton, during the First World War.*

Above: *Basil Hurrell, 1940s.*

Right: *Jack and Emily Hurrell, daughter Lily and grandson, also called Basil, c.1950s.*

Middletons

by Pauline Parsons (née Middleton)

My father, Gordon Middleton, was born down Lower Easton in 1908. He went to the Old School at Easton; Mrs Blythe was the head teacher. She was mother to Percy Blyth who kept the Post Office. Miss Bailey started as a young teacher there just before Dad left school. His father Albert Middleton wasn't born in the village, but he did a lot for Easton church. He was a churchwarden, when the Revd Bracecampe was there.

My father was married, and lived on the Dereham Road. He had two daughters, but sadly his wife died at 30 years of age. My mother, who came from Lowestoft, was living in one of the homes near Rose Cottages, with her three sons. Later her and my father married and they all lived on the Dereham Road. This is where myself and my brother Neil were born, and we have both lived in Easton ever since. We attended the same school as Dad. The teachers then were Miss Taylor and Miss Bailey. When Miss Taylor retired Mrs Pointer took her place. Two of my daughters also went to the same school. We have certainly seen some changes over the years at Easton.

Right: *Mary Middleton, 1987.*

Below: *Pauline and Paul Parsons at their wedding, with two sets of parents, Mary and Gordon Middleton (right) and Mr and Mrs Parsons (left), 1965.*

Bertie Mortimer and Family

Bertie Mortimer was born in Marlingford. He did military service and was a veterinary surgeon in the Army during the First World War. He also acted as a driver or teamsman using the horses for pulling the guns. After being discharged from the Army he returned to live in Marlingford. His wife died in 1918.

Harriet Wilken was born in Norwich and married Alfred Pease, whose father lived and died in Easton. They had three children, the first two being Alfred and Gladys, and the third child sadly died young.

Alfred died during the war aged 35 on 20 October 1918, just a few weeks before the armistice. Gladys' son Peter Duncan lives in Wicklewood in 2004.

Bertie and Harriet were married in 1921 and with the two children from her previous marriage moved into a cottage in a small yard next to Rose Cottages. Their family increased and the cottage became too small; in the meantime council-houses were being built on the turnpike (Dereham Road) – there were 22 houses in all and the family was allocated No. 2. For the move the funeral bier (two bits of wood on two wheels like a long barrow) was used to take the furniture to the new house. Bertie worked on a farm once again looking after horses and from there he worked as a lengthman, being foreman in charge of Easton and the surrounding villages for many years, until he retired.

Harriet was a hard worker and if anyone needed a hand she would always help out. She cleaned the church and the Church Room (known as the Green Hut). She lit the fires and was school caretaker and cleaner, all for 3s.6d. a week. She worked in the house for Revd and Mrs Jolly, helped at all the fêtes and children's parties and was always there to wash up and clear up after any village 'do'. She worked for many years on the land on various farms around Easton and also served tea and sandwiches in the agricultural workers' tent at the Norfolk showground for many years. Hetty, as she was known, was a very kind and loveable character who always had time for other people. Before many cars or buses were about she would put several other youngsters in the pram and walk to Barn Road in Norwich to the butcher's, get sixpenarth of scraps and walk home again. On many occasions during the Second World War, she put on a Home Guard uniform and stood in for any of the boys who were a bit the worse for drink. Most days she would be out with her old pram 'sticking'. People relied on sticks and wood for heating the oven in the wall, and for the fire under the copper to heat every drop of water that was needed. All water had to be carried in a pail from a pump, which stood on the main road amongst the council-houses. Hetty helped many people at the birth of their babies, taking all the washing home with her, and she was also with many people when they departed this life.

Bertie and Harriet had a large family of eight children – four boys: Gerald, Bertie, Leslie and Roy; and four girls: Betty, Margaret (Maggie), Irene and Helen. The family all spent a large part of their lives at No. 2. Maggie remembers that it was difficult at teatimes and they had to eat in relays.

We had three bedrooms upstairs, two rooms downstairs and a kitchen. We slept five in a bed. My sister used to cook a stew with pea soup lentils, she didn't soak them and they were as hard as stones, with dumplings like cannon balls; we laugh about it to this day. We had pheasants and rabbits if we were lucky.

Gerald, the eldest son, served in the Army during the Second World War and Bertie, the second eldest, was in the Navy for a time and then the Army. Betty, the eldest daughter, married an American serviceman and went out to America to live. She died in the USA in 1966. The other five children were at school during the war years. Of the eight children, five are now deceased. Bertie and Harriet had 21 grandchildren. Bertie died on 25 April 1962. Harriet died on 28 February 1974 aged 78. Both are buried in Easton.

Left to right: *Marjorie, Donny and Flo Mortimer, 1940s.*

Donald and Florence Mortimer

Donald served in the Army during the First World War and afterwards worked in London where he met and married his wife Florence. They lived there for a

Above: Left to right: *Maureen Mortimer, Derek Woodhouse, Beryl and Hazel Mortimer, Arthur Spooner, Pat Gent and Ronnie Spooner at Wells-next-the-Sea, 1945.*

time before coming to Norfolk to live at Little Melton, then moving to Easton into a cottage, near Rose Cottages, before finally settling down in a council-house in the centre of the village. They had five daughters.

Donny worked on the roads as a lengthman and also acted as MC at dances and social evenings held in the old Village Hall adjoining The Dog. Their eldest daughter Marjorie remembers going with her Dad to the dances and seeing Mrs Nelson playing the piano and a Mr Bennington playing the dulcimer. Maureen, another daughter, remembers seeing film shows there which the Home Guard organised and which featured Charlie Chaplin and other greats.

Donny and Flo, as they were always known, were a friendly couple and she never lost her London accent in all the years she lived here. The girls all went to Easton School. Beryl, the second eldest, grew a conker in a pot as a child and it got so big that it was planted in the front garden where it continued to thrive; it is now the large horse-chestnut tree in the centre of the council-houses on Dereham Road.

It was approximately 1970 when Donny had the misfortune of being diagnosed with cancer of the throat. He had a voice-box inserted with which he coped very well for several years.

Two of their daughters, Beryl and Mollie, have died. The three others are Maureen, Hazel and eldest daughter Marjorie Smith. Marjorie has lived in Easton most of her life in a house opposite her childhood home. Donny died aged 83 in 1983 and Flo died aged 91 in 1988. They had 13 grandchildren.

Outing to Yarmouth, early 1920s. The girl in the front is Marjorie Mortimer.

49

*Hetty Pease
1918.*

*Alfred Pease,
1918.*

Above: *Bertie Mortimer, 1948.*

Left: *Death Penny
presented to Mr Pease's
family on his death
during the First
World War.*

Left:
*Leslie
Mortimer,
1963.*

Right: *Gerald Mortimer, 1941.*

Below left: *Bert Mortimer (left)
and Mr Wilton celebrating a pools
win, 1930s.*

Below right: *Hetty Mortimer, 1962.*

🌿 Bert Mortimer's Family 🌿

Right: *Maggie Mortimer, 1944.*

Above: *Betty Mortimer, 1946.*

Left: *Siblings Maggie Lee (née Mortimer) and Leslie Mortimer in 2002.*

Helen Mortimer, 1963.

Irene Mortimer, 1944.

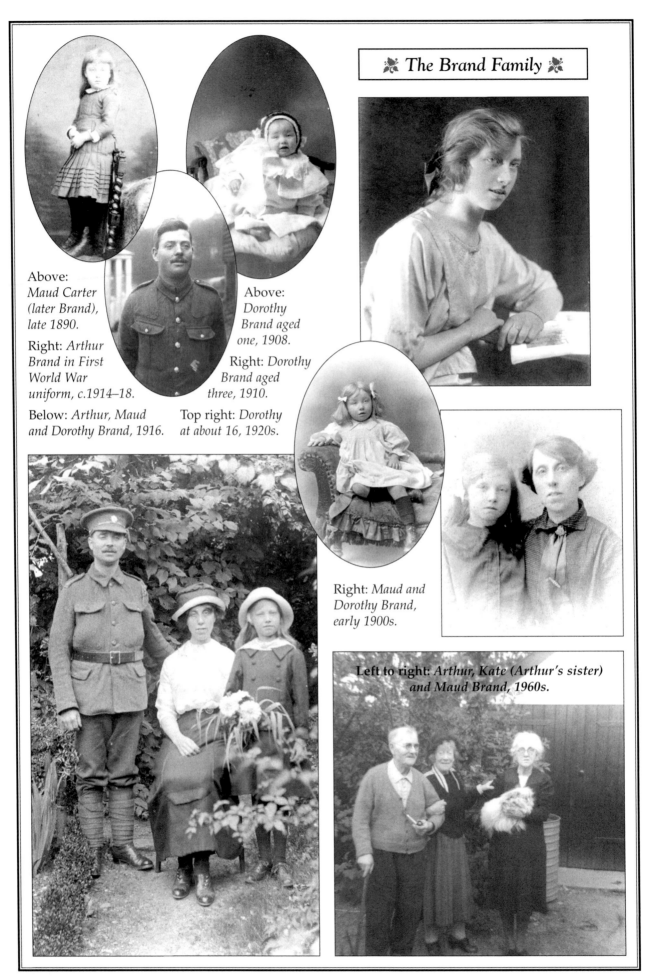

The Brand Family

Above: *Maud Carter (later Brand), late 1890.*

Right: *Arthur Brand in First World War uniform, c.1914–18.*

Below: *Arthur, Maud and Dorothy Brand, 1916.*

Above: *Dorothy Brand aged one, 1908.*

Right: *Dorothy Brand aged three, 1910.*

Top right: *Dorothy at about 16, 1920s.*

Right: *Maud and Dorothy Brand, early 1900s.*

Left to right: *Arthur, Kate (Arthur's sister) and Maud Brand, 1960s.*

William and Amelia Carter

When William and Amelia Carter came to live in Easton around 1890 it was to a small cottage – one of only two cottages on Bawburgh Lane at that time. He had a pony and trap that he used to take people to Norwich. They had one daughter named Maud, who was born in 1881. She often used to tell of her father taking her to Little Melton and tipping the cart over on the sharp bends. They would all end up over the bank in a field. Having relatives in London, Maud went to work there as a children's nurse. In the meantime she met Arthur Brand who lived in Marlingford. He also worked in London, as an apprentice cabinet maker with Rolls Royce. A lot of beautiful woodwork was put in their cars in those days. They married and lived in London for a time, coming to live in Easton in the second half of the 1920s, in the cottage next to Maud's parents, and moving into a council-house when they were built in 1933.

Meanwhile, William Carter had purchased a field in the centre of Easton. He had a bungalow built and lived there with Amelia until he died in 1938. Maud and Arthur then went to live at the bungalow with her mother. Amelia died in 1950 in her 99th year.

There were village allotments behind the bungalow. Arthur had a workshop built on another part of the field and carried on with the cabinet-making, producing some beautiful pieces of furniture. The carpentry side of the business also kept him busy. If there was a death in the village he would don his black hat and go to measure the body before making the coffin, and he also made many coffins for the various undertakers around. He employed village lads to help him with this, one being Bertie Mortimer (junr), who was apprenticed to him; before going home on Saturday at dinner time he had the job of clearing up the workshop. His younger sisters would help by picking up all the wood shavings, which would be taken home for Mum to burn in the copper fire on Monday morning. When the doors of the workshop were open many youngsters loved to have a look in, but were apprehensive at the sight of a coffin being made or the completed ones leaning against the wall. Arthur always had time to show them whatever he was doing. He gave up the workshop in about 1945. He died in 1965 aged 82 and Maud died in 1979 aged 98.

The carpenter's shop was sold, along with some land, to Mr Anthony Hogge, an accomplished wood turner who soon outgrew the workshop and had a much larger factory built back from the road. He employed many village lads in all forms of wood turning. He made a living in Easton for 55 years.

Arthur and Maud Brand had one daughter, Dorothy, who married Jack Sadd from Marlingford. Helped by his brothers, Jack built a bungalow on this same field, and lived there all his married life (this is the bungalow opposite the water-tower on the Dereham Road). He was a very well-known racing cyclist and won many cups and trophies in the 1940 and '50s. He also trained many youngsters in the sport. His best-known achiever was Beryl Cannell. He was a plumber by trade and after an apprenticeship with R.G. Carter he worked for many years for the Forehoe & Henstead RDC looking after the pump houses in local villages until his retirement. He died in 1983 aged 77 and Dorothy died on 1 March 1998 aged 91.

Jack and Dorothy Sadd's wedding day, c.1930s.

Maud Brand on her 97th birthday, 1977.

Easton Playgroup in the 1970s.

Easton Playgroup, 1970s. Father Christmas is saying goodbye to the supervisor Margaret Hobson-Frohock who lived in Easton.

Jean and Dave Ditton

I am writing about the Ditton family who have lived in the village for 40 years. Dave and I (Jean) moved here after living for a year of married life in London with my mother. Dave got a transfer with his job as a domestic-appliance engineer with Hotpoint. We have two sons and a daughter and one grandson and three granddaughters. Our oldest son Peter and his wife Sadie were involved in the Self-Build Scheme in the village, detailed in Chapter Nine. Our second son is an officer in the RAF and our daughter is a staff nurse.

When we moved up here from London it was so quiet and everybody seemed to have a bike. I also couldn't understand a thing anybody said. I worked in Jarvis' in St Benedicts before I started my family and then stayed at home. When the boys went to school my friend Phyliss Windsor and I started the playgroup in the village. We had only £1 to start with and gathered the parents round who were interested in starting the group. We had many fund-raising days and I remember that on the first one we only made six shillings. Many fathers made things for us, such as bookcases and tables, and Dave made the painter's easels that the children still use to this day. We asked for old chairs that schools had thrown out and had them repaired and painted. These are still in use. I went to evening classes (a pre-school supervisor's course) and college on a one-day course for a year. The playgroup was a great success and all the mothers had a hand in making it so. For a long time all the people who helped did not get any wage as we had to plough all the money back into the playgroup, receiving no help from the Government. Eventually I retired in 1977 after seven years as supervisor.

The playgroup flourished and continued to grow. I went on to be a pre-school playgroup visitor and went to different playgroups to help with any queries they might have. I also worked with Tupperware in the office for 27 years. Sadly, after 30 years, the play-group was threatened with closure as no supervisor could be found. I took on the job as a stopgap but unfortunately even with all the hard work by Denise Fell and Linda Rose it shut in December 1999. It was a sad day as the playgroup was an essential part of the village but maybe one day it will start up again.

Dave was involved with the Youth Club in the 1970s and in the 1980s he was a member of the Village Hall committee, at one time serving as chairman. At the time of writing, he is the chairman of the Parish Council, of which he has been a member for many years. The thing we are now both involved in is the Community Car Scheme which is designed to provide pensioners with transport to the surgery, hospital, dentist, etc. Now Dave has retired from his own business, Ditton Domestics, we sincerely hope to help the village remain a lovely place in which to live.

Goldsmith Family

Living at Lower Easton, Edith Goldsmith moved into a council-house with her two children when her husband died. She worked very hard to bring them up, doing housework, looking after children, working on the land and undertaking huge amounts of washing for the American servicemen stationed near here. Her daughter Joan was a very friendly girl with a bubbly personality. She was a Sunday school teacher for a time and served in the WAAF. During the war she met an American serviceman named Charles Ruby and they were married at St Peter's Church. Joan lived with her mother, and it was here that her first son was born, but when Charles returned to America at the end of the war, Joan followed as a GI bride and settled down well over there, enjoying a very good home and inlaws, and bearing two more children, a boy and a girl.

Several years later Steven, her eldest son, was killed in action in the Vietnam War, and approximately three years later Joan died suddenly. A few years after that Charles also died. Gregory and Joanne, however, survived.

Edith's son Herbert, Joan's brother, went to school in Easton and then worked on the land. He married Heather Sherwood, a village girl, and they lived in Easton in a farm cottage on Hall Road for a time, before moving to Brandon Parva for several years in order to be close to Herbert's place of work.

The couple came back to a bungalow in Parkers Close in 1955 with their daughter Gill, and Heather went to work at the School of Agriculture as a domestic for many years, whilst Herbert worked at Atlas Works, Lenwade. He died suddenly at the end of January 2001 and Heather passed away in February 2003.

They left one married daughter, Gill, two granddaughters and one great-grandson.

Above: Left to right: *Edith Goldsmith and Charles Ruby and his wife Joan (née Goldsmith), 1950s.*

Left: *Heather and Herbert, 1990s.*

Above: *Albert and Clara Middleton at the Vicarage in the early 1900s with two of their daughters – Nellie the eldest and Victoria. Their other children were Gordon and Cora, known as 'Happy'.*

Right: *Martha Barber outside the coal shed, at the house in Easton where ten members of the Barber family lived, 1932.*

Below: *Violet Rose Mary Lewington (née Barber) aged 19, 1947.*

Below: *Billy and Happy Dade's emerald wedding family group, 26 December 1986. Left to right, back row: William, Paul, Melvern, Sarah; front row: Greta, Billy, Happy, Janet.*

William (Billy) Barney and Cora (Happy) Dade

by their eldest daughter Greta Hanwell (née Dade)

My father William (Billy) Barney Dade moved from Costessey to Easton when he married my mother Cora (Happy) Clarice Mary Alexandra Felicity Middleton on Boxing Day in 1931. He was a plasterer and in his early married life he had a building business; he built all six bungalows, one house and one chalet on the right-hand side of the road going towards Costessey. He also did some work on Easton church. My parents had six children – three boys and three girls. Dad played football and bowls for Easton and later on he was the chairman of the North Norfolk Football League and darts captain for the North Elmham Darts Club. Mum and Dad celebrated their emerald wedding with all six of their children and their families on 26 December 1986.

My grandfather Albert and granny Clara Middleton first lived at Lower Easton and later moved to the council-houses on the main Norwich Road. My grandfather was Easton's churchwarden for a long time. He died on 18 March 1944 aged 69 and granny Clara died on 26 October 1961; both are buried in Easton churchyard. My grandfather Barney Dade died on 28 January 1940 and granny Sarah Dade died on 13 May 1971; both are buried in Easton churchyard. My mother and father's grave is in Easton churchyard also. My mother was 81 when she died in 1991 and my father was 95 when he died on 24 October 2003.

Violet Lewington (née Barber)

Ronnie, Daisy and myself are still alive but not living in Easton. Mother and Father are buried in Easton churchyard; Father died aged 67 on 9 January 1951 and Mother died aged 66 on 14 July 1952. The six youngest children went to Easton School. George, Gordon and Ronnie all served in the war. Gordon was in the Royal Engineers and served in Germany, George was in the Royal Army Pay Corp and was one of the first to land in Normandy on D-Day.

My family were Methodist and regularly attended the chapel at Easton until it was closed. We had a yearly outing to Great Yarmouth and were given a shilling to spend and a free tea in Regent Road. On Sunday evenings all the family used to take a walk to Ringland Hills. In 1937 we moved up to the council-houses on Dereham Road, Dad having left the farm. He then cycled to Norwich City Station where he worked until he retired. Mum did all her own housework, washing, etc., having a stone of flour every week, making all the bread. Life must have been very hard for her then, as there were no washing machines or hoovers, and an oven in the wall was all she had.

Billy Dade and Happy Middleton – the wedding group, 26 December 1931.
Left to right, back row: *Barney Dade, Dot Middleton, Gordon Middleton, Victoria Middleton, Albert Middleton, Phyllis Dade*; front row: *Ivy Dade, Sarah Dade, Peter Solomon, Billy and Happy, Clara Middleton, Bessie Bugg.*

❦ *The Barber Family* ❦

Above: Left to right: *Ida, Daisy and Violet Barber with the cottage at Lower Easton in the background, 1934.*

Top right: *Fred Charles Barber aged 19, 1932.*

Above centre: *Gertie Barber (née Secker), wife of George Barber and sister of Bertie Secker, 1935.*

Above: *Fred standing behind Queenie and Gordon Barber, 1927.*

Right: *Mabel Barber aged 21, 1931.*

The Barber Family

Albert Edward and Martha Barber moved to Lower Easton into a tied cottage in 1930, Albert being a cowman for Mr Kidner. At that time their eldest son, also Albert Edward, was working in London as a butler. The eldest daughter, Mabel Christina, was away in service, the second son, George William, and the third son, Frederick Charles, also worked on the farm, Fred driving the combine harvester. The second daughter was Queenie May who worked at Caley's Chocolate Factory – she was also in the Land Army before going to work in a Forces canteen where she met her second husband. Her first husband was Bertie Secker from Dereham who was in the 5th Royal Norfolk Regiment and was batman to the Revd John O. Dean of Easton.

Queenie and Bertie were married at Dereham church in October 1941 and were only together for a very short time, as Bertie's leave was up. Queenie never saw him again; he was taken prisoner of war and sent to the Burma railway, where he contracted beriberi sickness and died on 23 May 1943. He is buried at Kanchanaburi War Cemetary, Thailand.

Gordon James (fourth son) worked for Captain Maine of West Lodge, Lower Easton, as a handyman, and he then went on to be a painter and decorator for most of his life. Ronald Geoffrey (fifth son) worked for Mr Gowing at Honingham and was called up for service in the Medical Corp, with whom he went to Ireland and Italy.

The next daughter was Ida Gwendoline who, after leaving school, worked at the Howlett & White shoe factory in Norwich. The sister, Violet Rose Mary, who after leaving school also went to work at Howlett & White for a short time, then worked in the International Grocery Stores for some time before getting married and going to live in Mattishall.

The last child was Daisy May, who after leaving school worked in the same shoe factory as her sisters as well as Caley's Chocolate Factory and then married and went to live in Mulbarton.

Top left: *Queenie May Barber aged 18, 1937.*

Top right: *The wedding day of Queenie and Bertie Secker, October 1941.*

Right: *George William Barber aged 21, 1932.*

Mr and Mrs McCadden, c.1950s.

The McCadden Family

Mr and Mrs Bob McCadden lived in a farm cottage with their two sons and four daughters at the bottom of the two hills on Hall Road. Bob worked as a farm labourer and was also a pack man travelling round local villages selling his wares from his bicycle with a trunk strapped on the back carrier and various bags on the handlebars. He sold underwear, household linens and many other things and would bring anything you required the next time he called. They also had a small shop in the back garden from which a large variety of goods could be purchased. Mrs McCadden was very good at making wedding cakes, and there is no doubt that she will be remembered by many couples in the village for this.

Stephen Peacock

Back in the days of the Royal Norfolk Show of the late 1950s the local schools were closed for three days to accommodate for the event. The Wednesday and Thursday were the show days and the Friday was also included in this short holiday.

The main A47 road through Easton was very busy from early morning until midday and again from late afternoon until the evening when all the crowds made their way home. During the 1950s and early '60s the farm workers who visited the show all arrived on push-bikes or motor bikes. Living in one

of the bungalows which was situated next to the car park was a very convenient spot to earn some much-needed money. So our garden was opened up to take in bikes, which was cheaper and safer than leaving them in the car park. The front lawn was taken over by motor bikes, while push-bikes were all lent against the bungalow walls and fences to the side and the rear. Leather riding gear from the motor bikes was stored in one of the rooms, to save the riders carrying it around all day. By lunchtime when most of the people had arrived for the show, we had made enough money to gain entry in the afternoon as well as some spending money!

Above: Left to right: *Stephen, Hilda and Eric Peacock, c.1958.*

Left: *Stephen and Eric Peacock with the motor bikes, c.1958.*

Hilda Longbottom (née Peacock)

I was born during the Second World War and spent my early years living both in London with my grandparents (while my father served in the Army in Egypt) and our bungalow in Easton. However, most of my early recollections are of Easton – and in my mind it was always summer. As children we spent a lot of time at the old ford in Lower Easton fishing for tiddlers, which we proudly carried home in jamjars. Once I remember being chased in the river by a big black pike.

In the school summer holidays much of the time was occupied following the combine harvesters and building straw dens in the fields. As the combines grew ever closer to the centre of the field, everyone surrounded the final patch of corn waiting for the moment when the nervous rabbits would break cover. The idea was to catch one and take it home for lunch or tea. I caught one, but carried it into the woods and released it.

The school had a bell over the front porch. It certainly hurried your feet along Dereham Road when this tolled out. I found lessons with Miss Bailey in the little room – and a bit later Miss Taylor

Above: Left to right: *Glenis Bugg, Hilda Peacock and Pam Woodhouse in 1947/48.*

Above:
Hilda Longbottom (née Peacock) and her father on her wedding day, 5 August 1972.

Right: Left to right: *Derek Sparkes, Hilda and Doris Peacock and Margaret Sparkes, c.1939.*

toilets – 'with paper please Miss!' On saints' days we would all march down to St Peter's Church for a service and then it was the rest of the day off. I can remember lining up in class for a spoon of rosehip syrup, to make us healthy, also crowding round the table as the teachers opened food parcels from Canada or New Zealand at the end of the war. I was so proud to take my mum home a packet of suet and a tin of meat – my share of the food parcel. Some playtimes were given over to picking stones from the field to be turned into a children's playground, the jubilee ground now complete with swings and slides. On 5 November we always had a big bonfire behind the council-houses on the Dereham Road where the bypass is now.

In the winter we seemed to have more snow than we do today and had many happy hours sledging down Dog Hill. The heaviest snow was in 1947/48 which was the year my brother Eric was born on Christmas Day. When he was christened the snow was so thick that we couldn't get to the church so he was eventually christened in the Vicarage. The teachers could not get to the school, and the buses from Norwich ran as far as the Easton Dog but no further. The snow was so deep that we could walk on top of the hedgerows! People had to use the old water pumps as most of the pipes froze in the houses.

As there were not many buses in those days we often had to walk back from the Oval or Round Well after a trip to Norwich.

Much of my childhood was spent playing with the Sparkes children. Mr and Mrs Sparkes used to keep pigs, goats and chickens and their garden used to run right through to the field behind Marlingford Way. They kept the goats in a small field next to their bungalow. In the field there was an old air-raid shelter. Marlingford Way also brings back memories of the old crab-apple orchards which Mr Brand used to chase us out of; I still have some of these trees at No. 26. Sid Sparkes also had a field next to the White House where he grew potatoes and we would walk behind his tractor to pick up the potatoes for him. Another distant memory is of going to the farm where the Agricultural College is now with Pat Gent and helping with the milk bottling. The bottles would go round in a circle and it was fun topping them; there were no 'Gameboys' in those days! I can remember nervously flattening myself against a wall down there as some men struggled by with a huge angry bull.

There were many people who called around the village – the butcher, baker, laundry man, insurance man, milkman and clubman (who had a suitcase full of clothes and other nick-nacks). The mobile fish-and-chip van always had a queue.

It is good to think back to the old Easton characters and colourful nicknames – 'Darkie' Dix, 'Slicer' Smith, and little old 'Bea' walking her cat on a lead. Unfortunately, we will never return to a true village life but there are still the memories.

in the big room – very enjoyable. Each room had a big stove burning in it which regularly required stoking. The unenjoyable part was using the cold outside

Pat Wiepen (née Gent)

Having lived in Easton since the 1930s, we have seen many changes. It was a quiet place to live with only 97 houses throughout the village and very little traffic passing through, although we lived on the main A47 trunk road at around this time. There were always a lot of tramps on the road, men and women, mostly at weekends when they moved from one workhouse to another – the main one being at Gressenhall, near Dereham, and the other at Norwich, on the side of the West Norwich Hospital. They often came to our door with a tin and asked for hot water, hoping to get a spoon of tea-leaves as well.

Then the war years came along and at the beginning of the 1940s many airfields materialised around about. These were manned mostly by American servicemen. The Army also had bases around the area, one being a searchlight post on Honingham Brecks. We became friendly with a soldier named Bert West who was stationed there. He wanted lodgings for his wife and young daughter Jean who lived in London. They came to live next door to us, and we all became good friends; we still keep in touch with the daughter 60 years later. The Army also took over Model Farm and used it as a NAAFI, supplying food, etc. to local Army bases. We had plenty of traffic about then. The female Army staff working at the NAAFI were billeted with several families in the village.

Hilda Peacock and Jean West in gas masks during the Second World War.

The winter of 1946/47 was very bad. A great deal of snow fell and everywhere and everything was frozen up. Traffic from Norwich got no further than the church. I remember at home the water-pipes froze solid. We couldn't have a fire in the living-room but managed a small one in the front room. The house was freezing cold. This weather lasted several weeks. No coalman got through. When he did we were rationed to one sack to each house. We had to go into the woods to find something to burn. Then when the thaw came the snow had to be shovelled out of the loft (there was no felt under the tiles in those days). The pipes burst and water dripped through the ceiling – in most rooms we had pots and pans everywhere catching the water. The house was wet and cold for weeks. There was no central heating to help us then.

On the farm where I worked as a Land Army girl I met Theo Wiepen, who was a German prisoner of war and very young, as he had joined the army at the age of 16. He never went back to Germany again and was made a British Citizen in 1950. We got married in 1947.

In the early 1950s plans were made to straighten and improve the A47 through the village. The sharp corner near the church was taken off, removing the wall and several older graves in the process. Any remains they found were reburied in the churchyard and a new wall was built. The small wood on the Colton Road corner was also removed. Several families were moved from cottages near The Dog pub into new bungalows in Parkers Close. When 18 cottages were demolished to widen and straighten this part of the main road one other alteration took place. This was the removal of the top of the hill, which involved lowering the road in the centre of the council-houses. As the years moved on new houses were built in the village and traffic increased to such numbers that in the late 1960s it was almost impossible to cross the road, especially at weekends, when the holiday-makers from the Midlands would be coming or going to the coast. It was as if we had no right to be on that road. I remember one Saturday we had managed to get out of the gate, did our shopping and were in a lane of traffic coming home. Getting to our gateway we slowed and turned in. The car behind stopped and the woman (I won't call her a lady) gave us such a mouthful of abuse for slowing them up on their journey home. Traffic at that time used to be nose to tail – really dreadful. Over the years there have been many bad accidents on our stretch of road, and eight people have lost their lives, with several others being injured. It was a great relief to us all when we at last got the long-awaited bypass.

I have always lived in the village and Theo and I have four sons and one daughter, six grandchildren and one great-grandchild.

Pat and Theo Wiepen, 1997.

Gertrude Ethel Curson

(born 24 October 1898, died 18 October 1979)

Gertrude *(left)* was the older sister of Eva Tubby. She was a village character and was very kind and would do anything for anybody. She lived in Parkers Close with her cat 'Friendly' (who was in fact very fierce) which she took for walks on a lead. Gertrude would spend her days walking around the village with her old cart (pram) taking wood/kindling, which she got from the woodyard, to many people. She would also pluck and dress game. On her travels she collected conkers and gave them to the village children. She refused to have any electricity in her home and cooked on an open fire, going to bed with an oil-lamp until the day she died. Gertrude lived most of her life in Easton, apart from a short spell in Norwich during the Second World War when she was bombed out of her home on two occasions. She married a Hockering man but after a short time returned home to live with and look after her father. Many people remember Gertrude by her nickname – 'Bea'.

Eva Alice Tubby (née Harrowven)

Eva was born on 13 July 1908 in Easton, the youngest of five children. Her parents were George (Tim) and Emma, who earned their living as fish and provision merchants. When Eva was a baby she caught diphtheria which was a serious business, as in those days many children died from the disease, but when the doctor called the following day to find out what time she had died he was surprised to find her still alive. This was an early indication of the strength and fighting spirit that she enjoyed throughout her life. She used to go home during the lunch-hour from school and bunch up flowers for her father to sell in Norwich. After school she would collect four cans of milk from the farm for which she got paid 6d. from one person, 3d. from two others and nothing from another.

Apart from a short spell in Wiltshire in service she lived all her life in Easton. At the age of 35 she married James Tubby, a widower, and they had John a year later. They lived opposite The Dog on the corner of Marlingford Road until moving to Bawburgh Road in the 1950s. They still kept chickens on the land until James retired in the 1960s and the land was sold. This

Eva's confirmation, 1928.

was on Marlingford Road between Marlingford Way and St Peter's path next to the school. That allowed access onto land owned by Fred Bream and Victor Brand, which is now the Marlingford Way estate.

Eva loved animals, birds, flower books and all things natural, and continued to knit, read, crochet and do tapestries well into her eighties. She had a good head for figures and a good sense of humour but did not suffer fools gladly. Her remedy for illness was a drop of whisky and John said it was quite fitting that her last words were 'John, give me the whisky bottle'. She was very outspoken and would certainly have had something to say about the new residential development opposite her home. She had said she wanted to live to see her magnolia come into flower. Her wish was granted when she died at home on Good Friday 13 April 2001, at 92 years of age.

Left to right: *Bea, Eva and Edna Harrowven, mid-1970s.*

Edna Harrowven, sister to Eva, 1920s.

Left to right: *Nephew George with Eva and James Tubby, mid-1960s.*

Colin Hall

Coming into the village from an urban environment, one perhaps has certain preconceptions of what it will be like. A quiet backwater perhaps, a sleepy little place where very little changes, a place where the pace of life is so much slower. If that is the case then the reality does not match the dream. Easton is none of these things. It has, as can be gleaned from this book, seen a great deal of change and perhaps particularly so in the last few years. The new housing developments have seen people moving into the village from all over the country and they have brought their own priorities and aspirations. Easton is a village which does not approach you but rather waits for you to make the first move. You can opt in or opt out of village life depending on your wishes. If you do make the first move, however, you find warmth and friendliness and a desire to make you welcome. It does not perhaps have that community spirit which some other smaller villages have, but it is a caring community, which asks nothing of its new residents other than what they wish to offer. Do that and Easton can be a most pleasant place in which to live.

Cecil and Mary Bailey

Mary was a founder member of the Mothers' Union and on the Parochial Church Council for 35 years. She has lived most of her married life, of 64 years, in the same bungalow in the village. Her late husband Cecil worked for the GPO for 40 years as a supervisor in engineering. One of the larger jobs during that time was the supervision of the laying of the telephone cable under the English Channel, which met the French cable. He also organised the laying of the telephone cable in Easton.

Cecil and Mary Bailey, 1938.

Left to right: *Eileen, Cecil, Mary and Leslie Bailey, c.1977.*

Charles and Mary Sweet

Charles was a very good person to the people of the village and helped to get a lot of things done. He was a parish councillor and was also on the Forehoe and Henstead RDC. Charles would try to help anyone needing a council-house, and was often successful. The couple *(above)* had a car and would take people to the doctors, etc. – they were very kind. Both were on the PCC and Mary was a founder member of the Mothers' Union and took the meeting when the vicar was absent.

Bob Ponder

Bob was born in 1927 and was brought up in Easton and went to the local school. He said 'I had a good education at the village school. Miss Taylor was strict but she did a good job.' That's Bob Ponder who was known simply as Bob to hundreds of people.

He left school in 1941 and his first job was at the village dairy delivering milk to homes. He helped out at West Lodge for Captain Maine and family as boot-boy and gardener. 'The Captain was a rum old boy.' After work there was no social life for 15–16 year olds and, as Bob pointed out, 'we had no money to match the Americans or other servicemen that came to the village in the evenings.' When he was old enough Bob joined the Royal Marine Commandos and served his time along with his friend Arthur 'Woffie' Lee. He met Joyce when he left the Marines and they were married in 1954.

Bob was a farm labourer for several years before joining the Post Office delivering mail by bicycle. It was Easton in the mornings, and Easton and Marlingford in the afternoons. Later on when Colton was added to the round he was given a Post Office van. This was a great help, as it meant no more hills to climb. In between times he worked at the garage serving petrol. There was no self-service in those days. It was a busy garage and there was always a queue. Bob, who has always had a very good sense of humour, would have a chat and laugh with all the customers.

In later years the letters were sorted at Wymondham and Bob finished working for the Post Office. He carried on at the garage for a time but had to give up work through ill health. He still likes a drink or two and whenever you see him he's full of his old 'squit'. But then that is Bob as we have always known him.

Bob and Joyce, 2003.

His wife Joyce also worked at Easton Post Office for over 20 years and was behind the counter when a burglary took place a few years ago.

William Frederick Sharp

Bill was born at Green Farm in the village of Thompson, near Watton, Norfolk, on 12 December 1911. He attended Thompson School, where he was taught to play the piano and also won a medal for an essay on birds. When he was old enough he played for services at Thompson Chapel.

Bill was 14 years old when his family moved to Tuddenham St Mary, Suffolk, where they stayed for three years, and on leaving Thompson the chapel members presented Bill with a Bible. He went on to play the organ at his new chapel.

After leaving school Bill joined his father on the farm. While still young Bill, with others, drove cattle, on foot, 20 odd miles through Thetford to market. Bill also took the sugar beet to Mildenhall Station by horse and cart. Another of the moves the family made was to Langford near the famous battlefield, where they stayed for ten years, then moved to Great Cressingham.

Wedding group, 13 August 1974.
Left to right: *Jackie Fincham,*
Bill and Daisy Sharp, Thelma Kidd.

During the war Bill was conscripted into the Home Guard (he could not go into the Forces as farming was classified as a 'Reserved Occupation'). He and his family would walk or cycle for miles to chapel services at this time. When his father retired he bought a house at Carbrooke, and Bill then worked for Mr Crawford on a mixed farm for 22 years as a tractor and combine driver. During his time there he won a prize for hoeing as his plants were all nine inches apart, with no weeds. Around this time Bill bought his first car which opened up a whole new world for him and started him off with his love of old cars.

Whilst living at Carbrooke he met his wife-to-be, Frances 'Daisy' Scarfe from Easton, and this was when Bill was introduced to St Peter's Church and the churchyard! He agreed to tackle the overgrown churchyard and bought a new push-mower, attached pram wheels and eventually brought it into good order. For a short time he played the organ for services in the church.

Bill and Daisy were married quietly at Easton church on 13 August 1974 by the Revd John Bliss, with two witnesses present, Jackie Fincham from Carbrooke and Thelma Kidd, Daisy's niece. A wedding party was held at 14 Bawburgh Road for a few close friends and relatives.

Bill and Daisy worked hard for the good of St Peter's Church, especially with the Tea Caravan –

Daisy inside, catering and serving, with Bill supporting the venture. In the early days, when the caravan was parked at the house in Bawburgh Road, he used to tow it to the lay-by near the church (now part of a tree plantation) every Saturday and on bank holidays. After that it was parked in the Vicarage grounds. Bill was on stand-by for errands and odd jobs, and fetched water from the allotments, kept a check on the gas bottles and went for more bread and milk when needed. After chatting to customers about the ideals of the caravan, they were often given a donation for the church funds, and overall this fund-raiser did very well.

Bill developed an interest in vintage cars and joined the Norfolk Internal Combustion Engine Society ('NICE') and the Austin Ten Club; this hobby took Bill to lots of car rallies. He was so proud to show off his cars, winning various cups, medals and plaques and making new friends with similar interests. As he grew older these friends helped him to continue entering the car rallies. In the latter years he disposed of all his vintage cars except his 1935 Austin 12 Ascot, which he bought in 1973 and which, because of its age, became an historic car. It was in this vehicle that he took many a bride to church, also using it for special family occasions. Garaging his cars was a problem so he had a deal with Mr Litton, who allowed Bill to store the Austin in one of his lock-up sheds in exchange for Bill catching his moles.

Bill loved gardening but he would never hoe up a self-sown flower, even if it were growing on a path. Another hobby he took up after retirement was to concentrate on his mole catching, at which he excelled; off he would go armed with a spud (rather like a flat spoon on a long handle), traps, navy cap and green wellingtons. Not many of them got the better of him after he had studied their habits carefully. During this time he did a lot of work in Easton churchyard, cutting the grass and hedges, and it was a real credit to him – not surprisingly, he had many compliments from visitors to the church. He liked to take Daisy out visiting relatives, shopping and to the church, and he was a good taxi-driver to her.

Bill was also very talented musically; as well as playing the piano and organ he had a very good singing voice, and he would listen to 'Songs of Praise' and 'Sunday Half Hour' and sing along at the top of his voice.

If Bill had a fault it was that he collected and hoarded everything; he did not throw anything away which he thought 'might come in useful', as he

❧ William Frederick Sharp's Vintage Cars ❧

Left: The day Bill Sharp's Gressenhall Rally vintage cars went on a countryside run, 1999.

Right: Bill's old car, an Austin Sheerline, at 14 Bawburgh Road, 1980. The garage in the background was filled with spare parts!

Below: The Austin Sheerline, 1980.

Below: *The Austin 12 Ascot dressed up for the wedding of Haley Fincham, 3 August 1985.*

Bottom left: *A Swardeston wedding in 1986 with chauffeur Bill.*

Below: Daisy's sister Agnes and husband Tom arriving in style at Agnes' 90th birthday party held at the Village Hall, 1985.

Bottom right: Ken Wallace's Autogiro at a car rally at Reymerston, c.1980s.

Bill being awarded the winner's cup by the BBC Radio Norfolk presenter Roy Waller at Hingham Fête, c.1980s. He won the vintage car rally.

would say, and his shed and garage were bursting at the seams.

After Daisy died in 1997 Bill gave up cutting the grass at the church as age began catching up with him. His last job was to widen the long path to the church door as he promised Daisy he would do, and he also carried on with his mole catching as long as he was able. Bill had always kept cuttings from newspapers and magazines which were of interest to him. Now living by himself he concentrated more on putting them into scrapbooks in yearly order. He did not watch much television but would read his daily paper right through.

Sadly Bill died on 29 July 2001 aged 89 and he is buried with Daisy in Easton churchyard, which he had looked after for nearly 40 years. Donations given in lieu of flowers for his funeral were used to buy implements for use in the church-yard. Bill left a legacy to Easton PCC and this was used to install a microphone and loop system in St Peter's Church. It was dedicated by Revd Angela Reynolds on 28 July 2002 at the 6p.m. Evensong service

and was attended by Bill's sister Phyllis Warner, niece Gill Aves from Shipdham and Daisy's niece Thelma Kidd. Also on that Sunday a very grateful, hard-of-hearing member of the congregation, Mrs Beryl Hillesdon, made a memorial garden by the font as a 'thank you' to Bill.

Below: *Garden display (note the moles) memorial for Bill as a 'thank you' for the loop system in Easton church, 28 July 2002.*

❧ Frances 'Daisy' ❧ Eliza Sharp

Left: Daisy Sharp (née Scarfe) in the church tent at the Norfolk Show, 1991.

Opposite page: Daisy Scarfe, aged 13 in 1922.

Below: The church rondels in the east window.

Below: Group Trinity Epiphany party, Madera, California, 11 January 1981. Back row, third from left: Daisy Sharp; front row, second from left: Revd John Bliss.

Frances 'Daisy' Eliza Sharp

Daisy was the youngest child of Robert and Susannah Scarfe and was born at Marlingford Road, Easton, in 1909 (the house is no longer there). The family later moved to 2 Rose Cottages on the main Norwich–Dereham Road. Daisy attended Easton School and survived both diptheria and scarlet fever. After leaving school she went into service at Yaxham Rectory for Mrs and the Revd John Trevelyan, known to her as Father John, whose teachings would have a profound effect on the rest of her life. She became a devout Christian and also learned from Father John the High Church liturgy, which stood her in good stead for her future church duties.

Father John and his family eventually moved to Kennington, Oxford, and Daisy went with them; she was by now one of the family and helping to bring up the young Trevelyan children.

During the Second World War Daisy was called up to do war work; she did not want to work in a munitions factory, as her sister Agnes had to, and she was lucky enough to be sent as a cook to a wartime home that gave respite to mothers-to-be, some of whom had been bombed-out, and some of whom needed a rest from the Blitz. Some stayed a long time, others a few weeks, and small children also came with their mothers. Daisy always had a great love of children.

During 1945 Daisy was called home to nurse her own mother who was subsequently bedridden for almost 11 years; Daisy considered this her duty and did it with love. She worked very hard and with the help of her father they managed. The rest of the family visited whenever they could and to take over if Daisy needed to keep an appointment, etc. Like her mother, Daisy had a great sense of humour and had plenty of quips to raise a smile. She would tell the story of when, in the flood of 1912, the water overflowed the banks of the River Tud and was quite deep, and Mr Greenacre had told her that the butcher's cart had tried to get across the ford but being very top heavy with weighing scales, etc., it had overturned. The meat came off and floated down the river and Mr Greenacre (then a boy) had run home to get his dad. They came back with a stick and fished a big leg of mutton out of the water. They had meat for several days!

Her father died in October 1954. In November of the same year Daisy and her mother moved to a new bungalow in Bawburgh Road, which was so much better for Daisy. Her mother died in May 1956 and Daisy took over the tenancy of the bungalow.

Then began another phase in Daisy's life – she had her own home and found work in Norwich to support herself, cycling when she could. During this time she met William 'Bill' Sharp and a friendship developed. On 13 December 1963 Daisy was knocked off her Sunbeam cycle by a car when turning into Bawburgh Road. She was badly injured with concussion, two fractured ribs and a broken tibia and fibular at the lower end of her right leg. After she left hospital she stayed for quite a time with her brother Walter and sister-in-law Amy Scarfe at Thorpe St Andrew, who cared for her until she could walk again.

Daisy and Bill were married at St Peter's on 13 August 1974 by the Revd John Bliss with whom they were great friends; he was also Daisy's second 'Father John'.

Fund-raising for St Peter's was always high on the list of priorities for the couple. They worked in the church tent at the Royal Norfolk Show for as long as they were able.

Bill and Daisy used to staple the pages of the *Grapevine* magazine together and organise its distribution, as well as deliver many magazines themselves.

St Peter's School was also a part of Daisy's life – being a school governor for more than 20 years, and she also helped with the school library. She would hear the little ones read and was keen for them to learn their scripture at an early age.

The biggest project of all was in the summer of 1977, when a caravan was purchased for the purpose of selling teas and home-made food; here lots of ladies came up trumps with containers full of beautiful food every week. Very little was bought, just the basics such as tea, milk, bread, butter and sandwich fillings (unless they were given), with bottled gas being purchased to boil the kettles. Daisy kept the accounts meticulously and a profit was made every week.

Revd John Bliss left his parishes in 1980 to take up a post in America at the Trinity Episcopal Church in Madera, California, and he invited Daisy to go and visit him, his church and the new congregation. All was arranged and Daisy was taken to the airport; not only was she going by herself, but this was also the first time she had ever flown! She arrived at San Francisco Airport on 9 January 1981 and, being Daisy, she was soon taken to the hearts of all she met. They were also keen fund-raisers and took it in turns to invite Daisy for meals, have her to stay and take her sight-seeing. One of the trips she was taken on was to Yosemite National Park, famous for its spectacular redwood trees, and here she tried her hand at panning for gold. Lots of these newly made friends kept in touch with her after she arrived back home at the end of January.

Daisy cared greatly for her family, and she was the last of her siblings to survive; she had nine nephews and nieces – each one was important to her and they all loved and respected her in return.

On Daisy's 80th birthday a surprise party was held for her in the gallery at St Peter's Church, at which about 30 church friends were present. Her co-churchwarden Mr Peter Pease presented her with a crystal rose bowl, to which everyone contributed.

In April 1992 Daisy retired as churchwarden, and at the Annual General Meeting she was presented with a statue of Our Lady and a prayer picture and was thanked for her 18 years' service. She stayed on as a PCC member – she had already served for 40 years. She had also been church treasurer for several years.

Sadly Daisy died on 6 November 1997, and her funeral service was taken by Revd John Bliss who happened to be in England at the time. During the service Revd Bliss revealed that Daisy years ago had secretly paid for the lovely stained-glass rondels to be included in the church's east window. Mrs Elizabeth Bowlby, one of Revd John Trevelyan's granddaughters, travelled from Shrewsbury to attend.

Daisy left a legacy to St Peter's Church and with it was purchased a beautiful red leather-bound Bible for the lectern, the inscription on the front page being written by the Revd Jonathan Lumby and dedicated by him on 23 August 1998. Bill was also present, as was Daisy's niece Thelma Kidd, at what was to be Revd Lumby's last service before he left the parishes.

With the money given to Easton PCC in lieu of flowers, it was decided to put in a memorial window at St Peter's VC Church of England Primary School; the window (below) was designed by pupils Emma and Rosie Kemp and Thomas and John Larwood. It shows the cross keys of St Peter and a fishing net with its catch. This was dedicated in November 1999 by the Rt Revd Tony Foottit, Bishop of Lynn.

Thelma Dawn Kidd (née Scarfe)

I was born at No. 1 council-houses in Easton in the afternoon of Tuesday 5 November 1929, the younger child of Walter and Amy Scarfe. I had three older brothers – Peter, Arthur and Dennis – and attended Easton School from the age of five to 14 years and was nine when the war started in September 1939. It was to change our school life entirely. I remember so clearly the day Mr Charles Hart came to fit our gas masks – how I hated mine, it was so difficult to breathe. We used to have gas-mask practice when we would have to wear them for a set amount of time, and we did all sort of tasks 'to help the war effort'. If the air raids had been very bad at night, we had a little sleep after the dinner hour. Another memory is of the men and boys from our side of the road digging on the common at the bottom of our gardens to make dugouts for all to get into if Easton was bombed; it was hard digging for the men as it was very stony ground, and I don't know if they were ever used but we children had great games playing in them.

When I left school at 14 I worked for nine months at F.W. Woolworths at Magdalen Street, Norwich, which I was not very keen on, so I got myself another job at Wilson's, a fashion shop on the walk (gone now), as a cashier. I did six weeks' training at 12s.6d. per week and this was raised to 17s.6d. when I was trained. We did quite a bit with our earnings; we would go to the pictures on our half-day off which was Thursday, half-day closing. There were dances on Saturday nights and we went to the pictures again on Sunday nights. We had to pay some board money for our keep. A weekly bus ticket cost 3s.6d., but often the buses would not pick us up, as they would be full – there was not much petrol for cars then.

I had known my husband-to-be, Basil, for some time before we started 'courting', when he would take me to the pictures, etc. He had a motor cycle and he would fetch me from work on Saturday nights. One Sunday afternoon we were going to visit an aunt when a car came out of an opening on a bend at Hockering and knocked us off the motor cycle – we both suffered extensive injuries. When we had recovered from the accident we were married, at St Peter's Church, Easton.

Our first home was at Brick Kiln Cottages, Honingham, near where Basil lived, then we had a year at Hockering when Basil was a farm worker and worked for Mr Bona Law who died when we were at the property. We then moved to Quebec Farm Cottages at Dereham – Mr David Carey's farm – and stayed there for about three years until we bought our cottage at Honingham in 1951 for £750. We had £600, and borrowed £150 from Basil's father George and sold our Austin 7 car to pay him back. There were no mortgages in those days.

During the war Basil had volunteered to go into the Royal Navy; he went to enlist with Arthur 'Woffie' Lee who got in, but they would not take Basil as farming was a reserved occupation – he was very disappointed over that. He joined the Home Guard instead and then the Royal Observer Corps, and his mother saved all the money he earned from his duties for him, which came in very handy when we were married.

In the 1950s I lost the sight in my left eye, due to an accident caused by a nail rebounding when I was putting up a shelf in a cupboard, and was in hospital for 12 days and treated with the new sulphonamide drugs. In the 1990s I had two more operations on that eye which have helped a great deal.

Whilst at Honingham, Basil gave up farm work and started working for the Post Office as a postman, working locally at first delivering to Honingham and Colton. He was then transferred to Costessey Westend Post Office and then to Dereham, where he became a PHG (Postman Higher Grade), working in office duties until his retirement.

We have two sons, Peter James and David Martyn; Peter went on to Norwich City College and David to Hammonds Grammar School at Swaffham, which involved a very long journey every day for him. A taxi would pick the Hammonds boys up from East Tuddenham, Colton and Honingham and take them to Dereham train station to go to Swaffham. I did several part-time jobs when the boys were at school, including fruit picking when they were very young. Then I decided to get a full-time job in the city. I was successful and was taken on at Norwich Co-operative Society Ltd in St Stephens Street, and worked my way up to supervisor of a cash office. After our retirement Basil and I decided to look for a bungalow and found this one, 'Woodstock', on the Dereham Road. We sold No. 27 at Honingham and moved back to Easton on 1 October 1990, back to my roots, and next-door-but-one to my birthplace. All the family pitched in to help us move and we all worked very hard. Whilst at Easton we celebrated our golden wedding anniversary which was a very happy time. I was treated to a surprise party, although Basil knew about it. We have four grandchildren: Peter has two sons, James and Stuart, and David has two daughters, Sharon and Nicola. Nicky has a little boy, James, our great-grandson, who is a delight to us.

Then came the worst time of my life, as my beloved Basil died on 6 October 2002 aged 78. Our sons and their families are a great support and comfort for me.

Left: *A school photograph of Thelma aged 11 (note the Red Cross and clean hands badges), December 1940.*

Below: *Thelma Scarfe aged 16, November 1945.*

Above: *Basil Kidd and Thelma, 1946.*

Below: *Basil Kidd's retirement presentation and party at Dereham, November 1988.*

🌿 The Kidd Family 🌿

Above: *Golden wedding day, Woodstock, Easton, 7 September 1996.*

Above: *David and Peter, and,* in front, *Thelma and Basil, 7 September 1996.*

Far left: *Peter Kidd aged 13, 1960.*

Left: *David Kidd aged 11, 1961.*

Right: *Family group gathered at Basil and Thelma's surprise golden wedding party, 7 September 1996.* Left to right, back row: *Arthur and Dennis Scarfe (Thelma's brothers), Basil, Peter Scarfe (Thelma's brother);* front row: *Thelma and mother Amy aged 95.*

Peter Scarfe

Walter and Amy Scarfe's first child was Peter who was born on 18 March 1925. At nearly 79, Peter can recall his first day at the village school where he was taken with Jack Brand by their respective mothers. Life between then and the age of 11 seems to have been spent largely on the common at the back of the council-houses, playing games and mischief-making, although he can recall vividly the announcement of the start of the war in September 1939. He must have worked hard at school, as the combined efforts of Phyllis Bailey and Gladys Taylor were rewarded when Peter passed the 'Scholarship' exams at the age of 11 and became one of the few boys from the village school to go to the City of Norwich School (known then as The Red Cap School).

In the company of Norman Richmond, and later with Ronald Greenacre, he would cycle to school in all weathers and was never late. After a marmite sandwich for lunch and a full day of lessons and games they would cycle back home again, a round trip of perhaps 16 miles a day. There were only county boys at the City of Norwich School in those days but, being wartime, plenty of air raids and bombs. Peter prospered at the CNS, both on the sports field and in class (although he did suffer the indignity of alleged flat feet and also a broken nose from a hockey stick). When he left at 16 he was second in the top form, and he could and should have gone to university, but he realised that family funds would not permit this and he started work in September 1941. He declined the chance to go with a 'herd' to Barclays Bank or Norwich Union at £1 per week, choosing instead to join Larking & Larking, a firm of chartered accountants, where he was paid 15s.0d. per week, or as they put it, £39 per annum, which sounded a lot better.

He joined the Easton Home Guard, although he cannot recall handling a rifle! He also spent much time with his father on Royal Observer Corps duties (unofficial of course) before volunteering for Aircrew duties with the RAF. Like many others he was placed on 'Deferred Service' and joined the Air Training Corps while awaiting the call-up, which arrived in 1943, by which time, of course, the European war was well advanced. His main memories of that period were the regular football matches and playing a cup final at Carrow Road – the match was drawn, but his team won the replay. He trained to be a navigator, but this was cut short by a sudden complaint (a perforated eardrum) which 'grounded' him, so he finished his RAF days in the Pay Corps, mainly on the Gold Coast, West Africa (now Ghana).

This stood him in good stead because he studied for his accountancy exams on demob and qualified at the first attempt in 1950. He was placed first in the worldwide exams and won the Society of Incorporated Accountants Gold Medal for 1950. He attributed that success to his wife, Eileen, a Norwich girl who he married in 1945.

He later became a chartered accountant and was appointed a partner in his firm, from which he finally retired as chairman of the partners in 1990, just short of 50 years after joining.

He experienced air raids, bombs, fires, etc. whilst fire watching, and saw businesses crumble and others grow, whilst others were taken over. He also held various posts with his institute and his District Society of Chartered Accountants and became an active supporter of the Norfolk and Norwich Association for the Blind, all of which occupied a lot of his spare time. He filled nearly every post in the association and at the time of writing is the only individual life president thereof. After his first retirement in 1990 he began a new career and became a stockbroker with Barratt & Cooke, the region's local broker. His second retirement came eight years later, at 73, since which time he has eased down to a few professional assignments. The third retirement has not yet arrived! All this from his good start at Easton village school.

After 56 years of married life, he lost his wife; Eileen died in October 2001 and he lives in Cringleford in 2004. He has a married son and a married daughter and six grandsons, but no great-grandchildren – yet. Gardening and travel are now his main occupations, apart from work of course. He still visits Easton to see his sister Thelma, and catch up on village news.

Clockwise from above: *Peter Scarfe as a ten-year-old Easton schoolboy at No. 1 Dereham Road, Easton, 1936; on to the CNS opposite Rose Cottages, 1937; Peter in 1984.*

Dennis Angus Scarfe

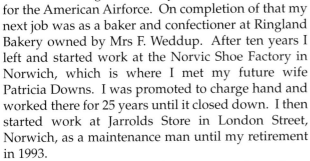

Dennis aged 17, 1945.

I am the youngest son of Walter and Amy Scarfe and was born on 5 February 1928. My younger days were hampered by bad health, until I left school. After leaving Easton School in 1944 my first job of work was in a canteen at Weston Aerodrome, which was being made ready for the American Airforce. On completion of that my next job was as a baker and confectioner at Ringland Bakery owned by Mrs F. Weddup. After ten years I left and started work at the Norvic Shoe Factory in Norwich, which is where I met my future wife Patricia Downs. I was promoted to charge hand and worked there for 25 years until it closed down. I then started work at Jarrolds Store in London Street, Norwich, as a maintenance man until my retirement in 1993.

I lost my wife in 2002 after 42 years of marriage. We have one son, Andrew, who lives with me at Thorpe St Andrew.

In my younger days I went to the Norfolk and Norwich Hospital several times. On one occasion, in 1937, when I was nine years old, I had trouble with my leg and, with no private transport, my mother had to take me on an Eastern Counties bus to Norwich and managed to carry me to the hospital in Newmarket Road, with many stops on the way. Coming back from the hospital with my leg in plaster, mother had to carry me to the bus station, but after a few steps she had to stop, as I was too heavy to carry. A bus conductor came along and carried me back to the station in Surrey Street and moved the people off the seats at the back of the bus and laid me along it.

Another memory of my childhood was the craze for peashooters; we got the middle stem of a bicycle pump and some haw pips and blew them at great speed down the tube. One day my brother Arthur, Derek Greenacre and myself climbed a tree almost opposite the Church Room and waited some time for someone to pass. It happened to be the church-warden Mr Herbert Middleton who came along, and as he passed we gave him a salvo of haw pips; he did not even flinch an eyelid, and we had a good laugh to ourselves. But what we did not see was him coming inside the hedge with a pail of water to throw over us. He got his own back with a smile!

Arthur John Scarfe

Arthur is the second son of Walter and Amy Scarfe, born on 18 October 1926. He attended Easton School from the age of five to 14 years and was taught by Miss Bailey and Miss Taylor. This is his story of three years of service in the Army.

At 18 years old in 1945 he was called up for 'the duration of emergency'. He reported initially to Nelson Barracks, then went on to the adjoining Britannia Barracks, where he was assigned to the General Service Corp. His first move from Norwich Barracks was to Kingston-upon-Thames to the Physical Development Centre as he was small in stature. From there he went to Bradford Barracks for Corps training for placement, and consequently he was designated to the RAPC (Pay Corp) and billeted at Manchester for approximately six months, where he was able to watch Manchester City and Manchester United football matches at Maine Road – Trafford Road having been bombed.

While in Manchester he met up with Ronald Greenacre who was in the Royal Navy; their mothers were great friends, so with letters from them they knew they were both stationed in the area. They made arrangements to meet at Southport, near Blackpool, which they did for two or three weekends, travelling by train. The next big development was embarkation and Arthur was shipped to Nairobi, Kenya, for about six months. Sitting in the NAAFI canteen one morning, Arthur felt a tap on his shoulder and a voice he knew said 'hello Arthur'. What a surprise it was to see Jack Brand – son of Victor and Vina Brand who lived almost opposite to him at Tall Trees in Easton – neither of them knew the other was in Nairobi at that time.

Arthur then travelled to Meerut, India, for around 18 months, where disease among the troops was rife, because of the heat. While serving in India he had earned a month's leave which was spent with other soldiers in the hills at Vice Regal Lodge, Simla, the Viceroy of India's summer residence, as a break from the heat. His unit was the last to move out of India, and Arthur was on duty the night India regained its independence. He left India late in 1947 and landed in Liverpool in January 1948 and found it extremely cold. The soldiers had to unload their own ship as the dock workers were on strike. After a home leave he went to Ashton-under-Lyme near Manchester to serve the last six months of his time, then transferred to York to be demobbed. He then had 56 days' paid leave money which he collected from Easton Post Office, then run by Mr and Mrs Percy Blyth.

Arthur aged 11, 1937.

🌹 Walter and Amy Scarfe 🌹

This image: *Walter James Scarfe aged 17, 1918.*

Left: *Amy and Walter with their four children, Dennis, Peter, Arthur and baby Thelma, 1930.*

A family wedding group, 1924. Left to right: Susannah Scarfe, Walter and Amy, Mary Margaret Sendall. Dora Taylor is in the front.

Walter James and Amy Marion Scarfe

In 1924 Walter and Amy were allocated the first of a block of council-houses to be built in Easton on the main Dereham–Norwich Road; they had to wait before they could move in, as in those days newly built houses were left to 'dry out'. The rent was five shillings per week, which was quite a lot out of Walter's wage. Forehoe and Henstead Council continued to build on both sides of the road, until there were 22 semi-detached homes; these houses are still standing today as they were well built, but they had no electricity or water laid on and the residents had to fetch water from the pump opposite, by No. 19 where Mr and Mrs Ponder lived, catching as much rain-water as possible in water-butts. Residents used oil-lamps and candles for light, a coal fire for heat and a copper with a fire underneath for the big weekly wash on Monday, a wall oven (also with a fire underneath) to bake with and oil stoves to cook on, in a very small kitchen compared to the rest of the house. There was no bathroom and only one toilet, which was outside, adjoining the coal shed. If they needed to go on any journeys they would go by carrier's cart.

Amy Sendall was born on 1 March 1901 at Frans Green, her family moving into Easton (Costessey Lodge) in 1914, the 'little castle' as it was known. Her father, John Sendall, worked for Lord Stafford as a woodsman. Amy attended Easton School for one year, from 13–14 years old, and then went into service to work for Mrs and the Revd W. Eugine Perrin at Easton Vicarage, now Diocesan House. It was during that time that she met and married Walter at Easton church. After the wedding there was a reception at Rose Cottages, then a happy evening was spent in the Church Room, where dancing and songs were enjoyed, and a set of knives were presented to the couple by Easton Football Club. Walter and Amy went on to have four children in under five years, three sons and one daughter, Peter, Arthur, Dennis and Thelma.

Walter had lived in Easton since being a small boy and attended Easton School at the time when Mrs Libby Blyth was head teacher – she was a very strict disciplinarian. On leaving school Walter went into farm work, then on to Moreton Hall estate as a woodsman, finally settling into work at Colton Fruit Farm, owned by Mr Colin Kidner of Easton. He did most of his training for this work at Burlingham Horticultural Station, where he gained various diplomas. The station later became the Norfolk School of Horticulture. He was promoted to foreman at the fruit farm, under the manager Mr Meredith, and although he started off with only one man

working under him (with whom he planted the first apple trees at the farm), the business prospered and over time many more men were employed there, including George Bugg and Jack Woods from Easton.

The main crops were apples, blackcurrants and a few loganberries, then later pear and plum trees were added. An apple-grading and packing station was established there which employed many female workers; Amy worked there for many years under Doris Blogg, the forewoman. The apples were graded for size then wrapped in squares of tissue paper and packed into light wooden boxes; in the early days the windfall apples were sent to Gaymers for cider making. In the winter several of these ladies were taught how to prune the apple trees, so were employed for most of the year. When not working on the fruit farm Amy also worked at Easton Egg-Packing Station.

Walter served as a school governor and churchwarden. He also enjoyed a game of bowls – at one time there were three generations of Scarfes playing the game, Robert (grandfather), Walter (father) and sons Arthur and Dennis.

During the war Walter belonged to the Royal Observer Corps. The station was on high ground at Honingham going towards Honingham School. Donald Greenacre and Mr W. Loseby from Easton were also members and would do a four-hour duty, evenings or night-time, on top of their day's work, but they were paid for the duties. Walter often did duties with a young Basil Kidd from Honingham, later to become his son-in-law. Walter was on duty one night when they tracked a strange object in the sky, which they reported into headquarters. It was confirmed that it was a V2 rocket which was later dropped on London.

In 1950 Walter and Amy, Arthur and Dennis moved from No. 1 at Easton to Colton. Mr Kidner had had two new houses built – one for his general farm manager and one for his fruit-farm manager, Walter. For 25 years Walter had cycled from Easton to Colton to work and back home again, so he was glad to be near his work. Amy was not too happy about leaving Easton, however, and Dennis had further to cycle to his work at Ringland Bakery, but Arthur had a motor cycle to get to his work in Norwich. The family stayed at Colton for 11 years until Walter retired early at 60, when they moved to Thorpe St Andrew, Norwich, which they liked very much. Dennis moved with them but by this time Arthur had married.

Walter and Amy had seven grandsons and one granddaughter. Walter died on 2 July 1973 aged 73. In 1982 Amy moved to a flat in De Carle House, Thorpe St Andrew, and lived there by herself for 16 years. A big party was held for her 90th birthday in Easton Village Hall. She died on 8 June 1999 aged 98.

❧ Walter and Amy Scarfe ❧

Left: *Walter at Colton Fruit Farm where he spent most of his working life, from the 1920s to 1950.*

Left: *Walter Scarfe during his retirement at Charles Avenue, Thorpe St Andrew, c.1960s.*

Far left: *Walter and Amy at the gate at No. 1 Dereham Road, Easton, early 1940s.*

Above: *Walter and Amy Scarfe going to a wedding, c.1960s.*

Left: *Amy Marion Scarfe, c.1989.*

Arthur Scarfe, early 1917.
He died aged 19 in the
First World War.

Robert Frank and Susannah Elizabeth Scarfe

Robert, known as 'Bob', was born in London in 1867 within the sound of Bow Bells. His parents – John Scarf (born 1839, died 1918) and Jane Elizabeth (née Jolly, born 1839, died 1916) – lived at Aldgate, London, where John worked as a dock labourer.

It was because of Robert that they moved to Barton Bendish in Norfolk and later to Rockland St Peter, as their London doctor said that the infant would not live unless he had the country air. Robert grew up to be big, strong and healthy, and at the age of ten he joined his father on the land as a crow scarer for two shillings a week; up until this age he attended school, which meant a two-mile walk and a weekly fee of twopence.

He met his wife Susannah Elizabeth Hall, born in 1869 at Whissonsett, Norfolk, whilst she was working as a cook at Scoulton Hall where he was also employed as a team-man working with and looking after horses. They were married at Rockland St Peter's Parish Church on 24 September 1890.

After living a good few years in a tied cottage on the estate, Robert changed his job and they moved to Easton in 1906 and there they spent the rest of their lives. They moved into a house off Marlingford Road just past the Old School. (The house is no longer standing, having been pulled down for redevelopment.) They then moved to 2 Rose Cottages on the main Norwich–Dereham Road, and here Susannah had a very busy life bringing up their two sons and six daughters. The children were:

Ellen Elizabeth	1.11.1892–22.04.1963
	(Buried in Easton churchyard)
Florence Louisa	2.07.1894–5.01.1978
Agnes	14.07.1895–15.02.1996
	(Aged 100 years)
Arthur	16.04.1899–20.09.1917
	(Killed in the First World War)
Walter James	24.06.1901–2.07.1973
Isabel Eva	16.04.1904–21.05.1993
	(Same birthday as Arthur)
Violet Maud	22.07.1907–8.09.1959
Frances Daisy Eliza	1.12.1909–6.11.1997
	(Known as Daisy)

Susannah added the name Eliza, after her own sister, on the way to Daisy's christening, therefore keeping a promise she made to her sister.

Robert was always in regular employment, sometimes walking miles to work; as a team-man he always had to be at work before the other men to feed and have the horses ready for the day's work. It was a very hard life for him. After his retirement, he was far from inactive and for quite a time he was an unofficial 'telegram boy' for the Blyths who then kept Easton Post Office. This duty involved him riding his bicycle on his round, and he was also very handy as a cobbler. He was a keen bowls player and used to play on the green beside the Church Room, known to the locals as the Green Hut.

During his younger years he had a most luxuriant beard, but he had to have it shaved off because it used to get caught in the horses' harnesses. He retained his thickish side whiskers, however, and for these he was very well known. In his latter years he spent most of his spare time standing on the path opposite Rose Cottages in the sun, passing the time of day with anyone that came by, or holding up his hand to those that drove past. He also spent a fair amount of time with his son Walter and his family who lived not far away. One of his regular duties was to fetch the water in pails from the pump next to The Dog.

Robert and Susannah suffered a terrible loss when they were informed by the War Office that their eldest son Arthur had been killed in action in France on Thursday 20 September 1917, aged 19. He is buried at the Tyne Cot Memorial Cemetery, Zonnebeke, Belgium. His name is also listed on the War Memorial in Easton church.

Unfortunately Susannah suffered a severe stroke in 1945 and lost the use of her right arm and leg, and was unable to leave her bed again. Despite this she was very mentally alert and delighted in receiving visitors. She was cared for by her youngest unmarried daughter Daisy, who was allowed home from her war work at Oxford. Susannah was able to hold a book and did a lot of reading as well as knitting – she had corks on the ends of her steel knitting pins to hold the stitches on, one needle held under her bad arm. She could also see out of her bedroom window and knew the times of the buses.

At some time during their early married life Susannah decided she that would add an 'e' to their surname, to distinguish it from a scarf worn around the neck.

On 24 September 1950 Robert and Susannah celebrated their diamond wedding anniversary. By this time their lives were very different from the days when, 60 years earlier, they had set up home on the ten shillings a week which Robert earned as a farm worker. At that time they could buy pork for 6d. per lb, beef for 8d. and cheese was $4\frac{1}{2}$d. (or $6\frac{1}{2}$d. for the strong sort), coal cost a shilling a cwt, with a discount if you bought a lot at a time – this was half a ton for

Above: *Violet and Agnes with their father Robert, 1925.*

This image: *Robert Scarfe, 1930s.*

Above: *Isobel Eva Scarfe and Maurice Brown, 1920s.*

This image: *Susannah Scarfe, 1920s.*

Susannah Scarfe outside the Rose Cottages, 1930s.

❦ Robert and Susannah Scarfe ❦

Three smart young girls. Left to right: *Isabel, Violet and Daisy Scarfe, 1915.*

Right: *Robert and Susannah's diamond wedding, 1950.*

Above: *Scarfe family, 1900.* **Left to right:** *Robert, Florence, Ellen; sitting: Agnes, Arthur, Susannah, Walter.*

This image: *Robert Scarfe, 1939.*

less than ten shillings – and three loaves of bread for 6d. Even so, that ten shillings a week had to stretch a long way! On the day of the anniversary almost all the family turned up, including nine grandchildren and six great-grandchildren together with friends and neighbours. Daisy was under strict instructions from her brother Walter to allow only a few people upstairs at a time as he feared for the strength of the stairs and floorboards in such an old house. There was a two-tiered cake, a drink for a toast for everyone, and tea and refreshments all day.

Robert died after a full life at the age of 87 on 17 October 1954 and is buried in Easton churchyard. Come November 1954 it was time for a compulsory move for Susannah and Daisy, this time from 2 Rose Cottages to a new bungalow at 14 Bawburgh Road. The ambulance service had to be called to get Susannah from her bed and down the narrow winding stairs and into the ambulance to move her to her new home. She was put into a kind of sling, and the family helped with this, but the journey down the stairs could only involve two men, one at the head and one at the foot of the sling – this was safely done, with only a few bumps. They liked their new home, with all the modern conveniences, and life was much easier for Daisy, with no more stairs. There was also a garden to enjoy.

Susannah died 6 May 1956, and she is also buried in Easton churchyard.

After the move in 1954 Rose Cottages were demolished to make way for the new main road through Easton, as we know it today.

Right: Arthur Scarfe's confirmation, 1916.

Below: The Scarfe family, 1920s. Left to right: *Violet, Ellen, Frances ('Daisy'), Susannah (mother) 1920s.*

Chapter Five

St Peter's School

St Peter's was built in 1857 on land given by Robert Fellowes for six children at a cost of £65. There was only one classroom but very soon this had been divided into two, one for the young children and the other for the older children, who eventually left to go to work at the age of 12 or 13. The school consisted of an entrance hall and the two classrooms, each with an open fire. The toilets were outside in the playground.

During our research we had the opportunity of seeing the old punishment book. This dates from 12 January 1925 and finishes on 10 September 1942. Presumably the nature of punishment at the school changed after this time. Of course we cannot name any children as their relatives live in the village today and some pupils are still here themselves. Below are some extracts from this fascinating document.

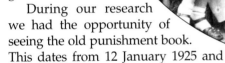

Left: *A group in the Old School reads a story, 1950s. Left to right: Lesley Harvey, Miss Phyllis Bailey, Ruth Simkin, Trevor Lee, Linda Kidd, Jon Kitchen, Phillip Sturman; front: Stuart Mortimer, Stephen Peacock.*

DATE	NAME	AGE	OFFENCE	PUNISHMENT
4.10.1926	Arthur ...	11	Insolence	2 strokes of cane
10.7.1930	Gerald ...	8	Rubbed hole in book and told untruth about it	2 strokes on hand
14.4.1931	Basil ...	10	Stoning a beggar singing near school	4 strokes on hand
6.10.1931	Dick ...	12	Cracking a nut in school	3 strokes on hand
25.11.1931	Thomas ...	8½	Said he didn't care after coming in late	1 stroke on hand
25.11.1931	Charles ...	8½	Catching and kissing and otherwise annoying 8 girls	Slaps on buttocks
21.1.1932	Gerald/Gordon		Treating girls disrespectfully	2 strokes each with stick
3.3.1932	Gerald ...	10	Cheating sums	2 strokes of stick
3.3.1932	Gordon ...	10	Allowing cheating	2 strokes of stick
27.4.1932	Harry ...	9	Telling wrong answer to dull boy	2 strokes on hand
6.10.1932	Herbert ...	9	Tickling boy's legs when answering question	1 stroke of cane on hand
28.4.1933	Harry ...	10	Dirty behaviour at urinal	2 strokes on hand
17.7.1933	Tom ...	10	Putting pencil up nostril and untruthfulness about it	2 strokes with stick
16.3.1942	Violet ...	13½	Singing a comic song while left to do needlework	1 stroke on hand
10.9.1942	Lawrence ...		Tore a double page from his Scripture book and stuffed it in the hedge	1 stroke on each hand

Above: *Outside the Old School in the late 1800s. The teacher is thought to be Mrs Sharp.*

Below: *Outside the Old School, 1902.*

These two photographs show groups of children outside the Old School in the early 1900s.

Above: *A group of children in the seniors' top class at the Old School in 1928.*

Right: *The front cover of the Punishment Book.*

Below: *Outside the Old School, c.1910.*

The Empire Educational Series.

Department

School

SCHOOL PUNISHMENT BOOK,

DESIGNED TO MEET THE REQUIREMENTS OF

Educational Department Revised Instructions

(APPENDIX II., SEC. 32).

JARROLD & SONS,

EDUCATIONAL PUBLISHERS,

10 & 11, WARWICK LANE, LONDON, E.C.

PRICE ONE SHILLING.

Further information was gathered from logbooks at the school. These date from 14 October 1878 to December 1992. Because the books are so detailed and entertaining we thought it a good idea to list some of the entries as they were written. Some of the names have been left out from this also. The school divided the pupils, in the early days, into standards 1, 2, 3, and infants 4.

1857	School for 5–15-year-olds. Population in Easton was 200.
18.10.1878	29 children attending.
1879	10 new songs learnt.
24.1.1879	Children's first Geography lesson.
15.6.1880	Lesson on the English Colonies in Asia.
3.5.1882	Half holiday, 40 children taken in a wagon to Norwich to see the Indian Bazaar.
8.11.1882	School closed upon the 9th and 10th due to the Mistress married upon the 9th.
16.7.1883	Report of Her Majesty's Inspector upon the school. 'The children have passed a fair examination, but the discipline might be better. The infants have been tolerably taught.'
28.11.1883	The new chancel of the Church opened and children attended both services.
5.3.1884	Infants' first lesson in knitting.
14.4.1885	Portrait of the school and children taken, children required to give up half last lesson in consequence.
16.5.1885	School closes for afternoon, Mistress went to Norwich to see Mr Garrett-Taylor, before he went away by train. She had been very much annoyed through Mr. ... (the late Master) and stated that unless a stop was put to his [proceedings], Mistress would leave immediately.
19.5.1885	Gave infants a writing lesson. Infants are very backwards. Some of them can not even make strokes.
22.5.1885	Mrs ... the temporary teacher, having been ordered to quit the school and Mr... was asked to undertake the charge of the school until such time the permanent teacher could enter on her duties. I must say the late teacher found a great deal of fault but sought no means to amending it, she neglected every standard.
29.5.1885	The school is not doing so well as thought. The parents take too much liberty in keeping their children at home for every little errand they require.
24.6.1885	Commenced school this afternoon at 1.30p.m. to enable children to leave earlier to attend a treat kindly given by the Revd and Mrs Blake.
10.7.1885	Gave children half-holiday owing to an annual feast held by the village.
11.8.1885	Bad attendance several children kept at home to look after younger ones.
2.10.1885	Several boys absent on Thursday (Brushing).
13.3.1887	School closed in consequence of Mistress having to go to Wymondham in answer to summons taken out against her for chastising a boy for disobedience and rude conducts. Case dismissed.
22.4.1887	Several children away this week due to Measles.
5.9.1887	School re-opened after harvest holidays. Several children absent (still working on the land).
1.2.1888	Absences owing to severe weather, some unable to walk to school due to chilblain feet.
14.2.1889	Holiday given for Valentines Day.
30.10.1889	Harmonium supplied.
15.5.1891	Boy absent this week with some kind of skin disease.
25.5.1891	School re-opened after Whitsun holidays. More children away with skin disease.
21.9.1891	School re-opened after summer holiday. Millie still unable to attend school also Brother William due to Typhoid fever.
17.6.1892	Diocesan Inspectors Report: having inspected the school I beg to report that it is in nice order, and the Religious Teaching appears to be quite satisfactorily conducted.
1.2.1894	Opened the school this morning with 15 children. Several families down with whooping cough.
25.3.1895	Only 22 children present this morning. Children kept away sticking (collecting wood).
1.9.1896	Inspector's Report. Discipline is satisfactory. Writing, spelling and written arithmetic are creditable. But reading should be more intelligent. An effort should be made to improve the reading and to cultivate general intelligence. The attention of the managers is called to the irregularity of the attendance. The new offices [toilets] have not yet been built. The present office accommodation is unsuitable. A classroom for infants would be a great improvement, at present they have no desks and their teaching lacks brightness.
10.1.1898	Received the sum of £5.10s. special aid grant.
18.2.1899	Received the sum of £4.17.6d. special aid grant.
18.9.1899	Inspectors Report. The practice of finger counting should be suppressed, infants class.

21.1.1903	*The school was closed by the Medical Authority owing to Diphtheria. Opened again in March being closed for 7 weeks.*
3.4.1905	*School opened and several children absent due to heavy fall of snow.*
18.7.1905	*Annual village fête holiday given.*
30.7.1908	*Only 12 children present this afternoon owing to Costessey Flower Show.*
1909	*The school was leased the Diocese.*
20.10.1911	*Absent children acorning again* [these were used for the pigs' food].
15.10.1914	*School closed by order of the M.O.H. Drs Nash and Lack. Another epidemic of Diphtheria.*
3.3.1915	*Owing to heavy fall of snow only 11 scholars attended. 3 sent home.*
25.6.1915	*New registers received from Jarrolds & Son. School closed owing to heavy falls of snow.*
24.2.1916	*Case of Diphtheria reported to the doctor.*
24.2.1917	*One case of Scabies. Authorities notified.*
25.2.1917	*Three girls commenced attending cookery classes at Honingham.*
24.9.1917	*School closed early to enable children to pick blackberries.*
20.11.1918	*School closed owing to prevailing sickness Influenza. Re-opened 4th December.*
31.10.1919	*School closed for peace holiday.*
28.5.1920	*Epidemic of measles broken out – school closed for a month.*
6.5.1921	*Exam for June Burser's held money for two candidates* (sic).
3.6.1921	*Miss Alice Hubbard supply teacher for the past seventeen years left to be married. Phyllis Bailey from Marlingford was appointed.*
3.10.1921	*Florence E. Hart commenced duties as Head Teacher.*
5.12.1921	*Medical inspection held and boy recommended for change of glasses.* [This is the first time that inspection for glasses is mentioned.]
15.5.1922	*Ringworm cases recorded. Five children sent home with letters.*
29.5.1922	*Nurse Large visited again this morning. The children with scalp ringworm are getting better but must not leave off wearing caps.*
15.6.1922	*School dentist, Mr J. Nixon called. On the 21st 8 children received dental treatment.* [This is the first time that the dentist is mentioned.]
12.7.1922	*Nurse Large visited again this morning. Ringworm cases not well enough to leave off caps.*
26.4.1923	*School closed for one-day holiday for the wedding of the Duke of York.*
6.7.1923	*School closed for Sunday school treat to Great Yarmouth.*
9.10.1925	*The school Medical Inspector, Dr Davidson, held a medical examination today. 38 children examined 4 sent home with dirty heads and 5 to go to the eye infirmary.*
13.5.1927	*School dentist visited this morning and treated five children with bad teeth.*

Group of children in the juniors' small class at the Old School, 1928.

20.12.1928	*The timetable will not be strictly adhered to this afternoon, as it is an open day for the parents.* [This is the first time that a parent day is mentioned.]
18.9.1930	*Dr Agnew called and left papers re: the serving of fresh milk to scholars at 1p per bottle. 6 only agreed to take it as Horlicks malted milk is already served in the cold weather.*
25.7.1932	*Several cases of Measles. The infants' class has been excluded from the school for the rest of the week owing to outbreak.*
28.9.1932	*Nurse inspected the school again excluded 2 children for having their heads in a verminous condition and another with impetigo.*
11.11.1932	*Two minutes' silence was observed.*
1.12.1933	*Miss Gladys Taylor took up duties as Head Teacher in the school.*
24.5.1934	*An Empire Day lesson will be given to the assembled school this morning.*
16.11.1934	*Boys reported suffering from mumps.*
21.11.1934	*9 more pupils have been excluded for colds, sore throats and swollen glands.*
22.11.1934	*4 more pupils suffering with mumps.*
23.11.1934	*2 more sent home with swollen neck and face.*
28.11.1934	*School closes for two days.*
-.11.1934	*Duke of Kent's wedding.*
3.5.1935	*School closed for two days holiday for Silver Jubilee.*
13.5.1935	*Peter Scarfe (1 year early) and Leslie Tuck have gone to the Education Office for the oral exam for Junior Scholarship.*
11.7.1935	*Miss Taylor attended refresher course at Norwich Training College.*
6.1.1935	*School closed all day on the occasion of the wedding of the Duke of Gloucester.*
28.1.1936	*School closed all day on the occasion of the funeral of the late King George V.*
7.9.1936	*65 pupils on the register. Three teachers.*
-.1.1937	*Head teacher and supply teacher both ill, this left Miss Bailey, the infant teacher, with 65 children.*
11.5.1937	*School closed for Coronation holiday and Whitsun holiday, to re-open 19th May. The piano from village hall was brought into school for our use.* [The harmonium had given up.]
5.9.1938	*Girl in Dereham Hospital in isolation suffering with Scarlet Fever.* [She was one of the first patients to go to Dereham as it was new.]
28.9.1938	*Every child has been fitted with a respirator this afternoon. Children were helped with the fitting of gas masks.*
-.2.1939	*Piano tuner called and tuned both piano and harmonium.*
1.9.1939	*There are five children attending who have been evacuated from Tottenham under the government scheme on the outbreak of war.*
29.1.1940	*Head teacher late for school having had to dig way through snowdrift on road.* [This is the time Freddie Fox did his sledging.]
7.2.1940	*A warning has been issued that the enemy is dropping toy balloons filled with gas in this area. Children told.*
18.10.1940	*Children spent morning in the wood collecting sticks and cones for the cottages given over to evacuees.*
29.5.1941	*Dr Johnson treated 46 children for diphtheria immunisation.*
19.3.1942	*School closed, as there was no coal.*
29.4.1942	*School is being used as a rest centre following severe air raids on Norwich.*
4.5.1942	*While school is being used as rest centre it is impossible to start at 9a.m. as the rooms cannot be thoroughly cleaned and aired in time.*
11.9.1942	*School closed for two weeks for fruit picking and potato lifting.*
7.9.1942	*Children have again been warned against touching strange objects, which may contain explosives.*
25.3.1943	*Inquiry as to possibility of having hot meals served to children at mid-day. Parents asked to consider this.*
23.2.1944	*8 pairs of Wellington Boots the gift of the American Red Cross were delivered.*
19.7.1944	*Mr Durrell, Home Farm, has applied for help from the school for blackcurrant picking.*
25.7.1944	*6 evacuees have been admitted today.*
3.10.1944	*Mr Durrell, Home Farm, has applied for help with his potato picking.*
9.4.1945	*40 Norfolk children on books* [register] *and 3 evacuees.*
20.9.1945	*Chairman, Managers and Revd Frost called this morning in connection with the completion of new heating installation.*
15.4.1946	*11 cases of measles reported. School closed next day for the three weeks.*
16.9.1946	*Milk delivered in ⅓-pint bottles and will be free.*
11.2.1947	*School closed due to road blocked by deep snow.*

Above: *Old School group with teachers Miss Bailey (left) and Miss Taylor (right), 1947.*

Right: *Teachers at the Old School. On the left is Miss Taylor and on the right is Miss Bailey, 1933.*

Below: *School outing in 1949. Left to right, back row: Doreen Ponder, Michael Dixon, Mrs Bailey; front row: Polly Lamb, Molly Parsons, Helen Frost, Sylvia Middleton, Hilda Peacock, Pat Stevenson.*

School outings for girls and boys in the 1950s or '60s.

Above: *A group in the playground of the Old School with Miss Bailey, early 1950s.*

Right: *A group outside the Old School in the 1950s.*

Below: *Inside the Old School in the big room, in 1954, with teachers Miss Bailey (left) and Mrs Pointer (right).*

Children dressed up for Empire Day, early 1930s.
Left to right: *Ronald Chapman, Nancy Sherwood, Jack Brand, Marjorie Mortimer, Herbert Goldsmith, Gerald Mortimer.*

Below: *School outing for the older girls and boys, 1947. Left to right, front row: Helen Frost, Hilda Peacock, Molly Parsons, Helen Mortimer, ? Heriot, Sylvia Middleton, Muriel Barber.*

Above: *Children outside the Old School, 1971.*

18.2.1947	*Due to fuel crises in the country all children in one classroom.*
4.7.1947	*We have received 5 country dance records.*
7.10.1947	*The blackout material cloth and wire netting was removed from the school windows after the war.*
20.11.1947	*School is closed for two days holiday on the occasion of the marriage of HRH Princess Elizabeth.*
26.4.1948	*Half-day holiday to celebrate the Silver Wedding of their Majesties, King George VI and Queen Elizabeth.*
1949	*School became Voluntary Controlled.*
11.1.1949	*Number of children on books is 36.*
2.2.1949	*Load of firewood delivered from Easton Woodworkers Ltd. 17/6d (was 15/-). It has been reported to Miss Bailey that children should not lose their lesson time fetching a bucket of drinking water. On this occasion they went to the Council House pump because the nearer pump was not usable. The cleaner will be asked to get a bucket of water every morning.*
12.9.1949	*Hilda Peacock was successful in the Norfolk Secondary Schools Examination and has left us for Dereham High School for Girls.*
24.4.1950	*School has been decorated and repaired during the holidays. There are 40 children on the books.*
19.1.1951	*Many children down with colds, influenza and mumps.*
27.7.1951	*Attendance low due to epidemics of mumps and chicken pox.*
4.12.1951	*First meal was served in this school, from their own kitchen.*
15.2.1952	*We shall listen to the broadcast programmes during the funeral procession and burial service for the King during the day, and observe 2 minutes silence in his memory at 2p.m.*
6.5.1952	*His Majesty King George VI died today.*
12.6.1952	*Milk now delivered in pint bottles to be distributed.*
25.6.1952	*School closed for Royal Norfolk Show* [continues for many years].
12.1.1953	*There are 49 children on the books.*
19.5.1953	*50 Coronation Souvenir New Testaments arrived from Norfolk Education Office.*
29.5.1953	*School closed for Coronation celebrations.*
15.6.1953	*Water has been laid on in the School.*
9.10.1953	*19 children down with whooping cough.*
1954	*School began to take infants and juniors only.*
1.2.1954	*New stove fitted in Senior Room.*
6.9.1955	*New stove in infants' room. 41 children on the books.*
20.7.1956	*School closed for two days for blackcurrant picking.*
30.5.1957	*District sports held at the New Costessey Junior School.*
10.2.1958	*Several children down with mumps.*
26.2.1958	*School closed owing to severe snow conditions few buses can reach here.*
20.7.1959	*Outing to Norwich Castle.*
6.9.1960	*Mr Greenwood came to discuss school equipment and see children work. He remarked upon the very white school floor and complimented the caretaker on its cleanliness.*
13.12.1962	*Gift presented to Miss Bailey on the occasion of her retirement.*
21.10.1964	*Bring and buy sale for Oxfam.*
11.1.1966	*42 children on the books.*
10.9.1968	*Mrs Weaver becomes Head Teacher.*
11.10.1968	*First time Keep Fit started in the evenings.*
1969	*School became a first school for children aged 4–8 years.*
23.1.1969	*PC Brackpool presented cycling proficiency certificates for the first time.*
3.6.1969	*Children started swimming instruction at Costessey School.*
8.9.1970	*51 children attending school.*
29.10.1970	*Mrs Mortimer leaves after working in the school for 20 years.*
5.2.1971	*Children watched two men walk on the moon.*
15.2.1971	*Decimal Day: £.s.d. becomes £ and pence.*
7.9.1971	*Mobile classroom erected in field. Miss Cole (now Mrs Blathwayt) now in charge of the reception class in the mobile.*
21.12.1971	*Mrs Weaver took Barbara Stapleton and Timothy Frost to reception given by the Lord Mayor at Shire Hall Norwich.*
11.3.1972	*Graham O'Dell was killed in a road accident on his way across the A47 by the church.*
21.3.1972	*School was closed Tuesday afternoon during the funeral of Graham. Mrs Weaver played the organ.*
14.1.1973	*School had a day's holiday to celebrate Princess Anne's wedding to Captain Mark Phillips.*
11.4.1973	*41 children attending school. The building of the new school has begun.*
8.2.1974	*MOVED INTO THE NEW SCHOOL BUILDING. IT WAS A DAY OF GREAT EXCITEMENT.*

10.9.1974	Boy absent. As I wondered if he was playing truant, Mrs Steward took his reading book to his home to enquire how he was and to suggest that he might manage to read some of his book when he felt better. His Mother said she had sent him to school. After about 10mins searching and calling for him he was found hiding under the bed. Welfare Officer informed.
21.11.1974	I advised Mrs … that she must hold Sharon's hand when crossing the busy A47. Four parents had reported that she held dog lead in one hand, the little boy in the other and left Sharon to cross on her own. I suggested she leave the dog at home.
17.1.1975	Revd Bliss conducted a simple service of dedication for the bench seat which Mr and Mrs O'Dell had given the school in memory of Graham. Mr Roy made the seat.
15.7.1976	Mr Ward gave a talk and film show on Green Cross Code of Road Drill.
7.9.1976	45 children on register.
3.6.1978	Scholars were presented with Jubilee pen and mug to commemorate Her Majesty's Silver Jubilee.
20.12.1978	Miss Bingham called to wish Mrs Weaver a long and happy retirement. This was Mrs Weaver's last day. [She was headmistress for ten years.]
15.2.1979	Very heavy snow falls throughout the country. The A47 blocked in some places.
-.12.1980	Increasing problem of parents coming into school in the mornings. Today last parent was asked to leave at 9.35a.m.
-.11.1981	Held own bonfire in school grounds. Parents came, we had hot dogs and chocolate.
5.1.1983	41 children attending school.
17.1.1983	Workmen came to mend the leaking roof. They discovered that thieves had removed the lead flashing and the snow had blown in.
19.12.1983	All the children sang carols to the Good Companions.
17.2.1984	I accompanied eight fourth year children to the County Music Festival in Saint Andrew's Hall. The children played two recorder pieces accompanied by percussion instruments.
22.4.1985	A PTA meeting was held at 8.00p.m. and it was decided unanimously that the PTA should now be known as The Friends of Easton School so as to include grandparents, parents of past pupils and other interested people in supporting the activities of the village school.
10.5.1985	Parents, children, teachers, past pupils, governors and villagers came to the official re-hanging ceremony of the Old School Bell. Mr Spinks (parent) made a new bell cover and Mr Thomas Greenacre being the oldest living ex-pupil of Easton School rang the bell.
24.5.1985	This is the last day that meals will be cooked on the premises. From Monday June 3rd meals will be brought in containers from Costessey Junior School.
1.7.1987	School closed for the Norfolk Show. This will be the last time it is permitted before the new national legislation ends all such breaks.
16.10.1987	Hurricane force winds devastated our grounds. At least 8 trees were blown down and many trees lost branches. Fallen trees blocked roads and the danger out of doors was too great so that we had to close the school. Luckily the building was not damaged.
30.10.1987	British Trust for Conservation came and brought 80 young trees which the children helped to plant in the woodlands.
22.1.1988	Today we had our new computer set up for the children to use.
12.12.1989	Performance of Christmas Entertainment to which the playgroup, Toddler Group and Easton Good Companions were invited.
5.1.1991	42 children on roll.

Group of children in the Old School saying goodbye to Maggie Mortimer the dinner lady, c.1970.

Above: *Easton School, 1947/48.* Left to right, back row: *Ivan Shingles, Gloria Seaman, Ivor Bugg;* front row: *Muriel Barber, Polly Lamb, Hilda Peacock.*

Right: *Letter from Thelma Scarfe to her Aunt Daisy, 1940.*

Below right: *Invitation to the opening of the New School.*

Below: *Mrs Walpole, the oldest living ex-pupil of the Old School, and the youngest pupil, Adrian Gaskin, when the school moved into the new building, 1974.*

Bottom: *The site for the New School before any building took place, early 1970s.*

Above: *Last class from the Old School, 1973.*
Left to right, back row: *Lawrence Abel, Robert Ditton, Stephen Cossey.*

Below: *First children in the New School, 1974.*

There are a few pupils from the 1930s who well remember the Old School and have the following tales to tell.

Clarice Kidd

All the children had to do needlework, and one day I lost my needle. All through the lesson I pretended to sew. The teacher would have told me off if she had found out. I only told Mum about it.

Pat Wiepen

The teacher in my time was Miss Taylor; she was very strict and we had scripture every morning or reading from the Bible. I don't remember much of the little class, only that we first heard of Snow White as the teacher read the story to us. There were always hymns, sums and reading. We did country dancing and Maypole dancing – the boys didn't like it. Sometimes our parents came to watch us.

During the war we had the playground dug up for a garden, and we all tended the vegetables and did the weeding – we all did something. One day some of the boys brought in snails from the garden. Bob Harrowven made us giggle as he brought them in tucked in his pocket. The teacher asked what we were laughing at. It was because he had put them into her needlework bag and they were all crawling out. She wasn't too pleased.

When going to or from home to school we had to stay on the side of the road we lived on and walked in between two ropes as we never had any footpaths. We always carried our gas mask and if the siren went we got into the ditch.

After school there was always plenty of things to do. We collected rose-hips from the hedges to be made into rose-hip syrup and picked up acorns for the pigs. There was a large common where the air-raid trenches were. We played lots of games on there or a paper-chase through one of the many woods. I think top and whip in Bawburgh Lane was a great favourite for lots of us. In the summer we would spend many hours down by the river having a paddle and catching tiddlers in a jamjar.

Freddie Fox

I remember the time when the teacher was late for school due to the weather so we all went down Dog Hill sledging. When she arrived and found out she soon came down and caught us. I also got the cane for taking out the sting from bees and chasing the girls with them. I put carbine in the inkwells and that made them all froth up, I had to stand in the corner and got the cane again. One boy in the classroom put a bullet in the fire and blew the fire out. The boys all had to knit for the war, helmets and gloves for the soldiers, also thick helmets for the Russians. We all used to ask the girls to help us on the difficult bits without the teacher knowing.

Joan Chapman

I was six years old when I started school – that is when my sister and I moved to Easton. Religion seemed to have taken a big part in school life. What I remember was register, prayer, a hymn then a lesson in scripture. Every so often we took an exam with Mr Beale the Diocesan Inspector. Miss Taylor was a very religious person and she took me through the lessons we had before I was confirmed as our vicar was in the Army. Miss Bailey, who was the infants' teacher in 1921, was still there when my children went to school in the late 1950s. I can still see her on her bike coming up Marlingford Road. I remember singing in the choir at the church and being paid one shilling at the wedding of Marion Kidner; it was ever so posh and we had to be on our best behaviour.

Thelma Kidd

During the war our education took a tumble, and the curriculum was followed. When the air raids took place on Norwich we often had a sleep at school. We collected waste paper and cardboard – all we could lay our hands on – and stored it in the boys' cloakroom.

Ron Greenacre

As best as my memory serves me, the highlights of school started with the Maypole dance, which we did on May Day. I remember the ribbons making patterns as we danced in and out of the circle but, like most boys, I hated it. Occasionally there was a school outing although I can only really recall one to London to see St Paul's Cathedral in the morning and Regents Park zoo in the afternoon. Sometimes in the summer we went to the coast. Once we went to Wells and the Revd Dean was most upset because it was arranged for a Sunday. At Christmas there was always a combined school and Sunday school party. This was held in the Green Hut and each child received a gift of some sort. Father Christmas was generally Charlie Hart, the churchwarden, who lived in the bungalow next to the Vicarage.

The New School was built in 1973 approximately 100 meters from the old one on the other side of the road, and the whole school moved on 8 February 1974. It is now called St Peter's First School. The head-mistress then was Mrs Weaver. The children numbered about 40 and were all under the age of eight. From Easton they went out of the village to various schools, the main one being in Costessey. The New School was much bigger, much lighter and had all the mod cons, such as a big kitchen, rooms for the headmistress and staff, a main hall for activities and, last but not least, indoor toilets.

The school football team, 1990s.

Hilary Kirby, Headmistress, 1993–2002

I took over the headship of St Peter's First School in January 1993 and retired in August 2002, a period of ten years minus one term. These were years of sweeping changes in education nationally – devolved budgets to schools, the introduction of the National Curriculum's testing of pupils at 7 and 11 years in English, maths and science, OFSTED inspections and the literacy and numeracy strategies.

Whilst putting all the Government directives into place we had great changes at Easton; the change from first to primary school, a large, innovative, purpose-built new building and an increase in pupil numbers. I inherited a school with 46 pupils aged 4–7, who transferred to Costessey Junior School for the rest of their primary schooling, in a tiny Portakabin-like building with two classrooms, an office and a small group room. For assemblies, PE and lunch we moved a screen back from Mrs Pease's class to accommodate the whole school. There was a part-time teacher to give me office time, a classroom assistant, secretary, caretaker, dinner lady and parent helpers.

Then in 1994 came the first news of change. Norfolk County Council intended to close Honingham Primary School, as pupil numbers there were falling sharply, and bus children from the villages of Honingham, East Tuddenham and Colton to Easton School, which would become a 4–11 primary school. Of course, governors and parents of Honingham School fought the closure but at the beginning of June 1995 I received a phone call telling me that the closure would go through and that we would become a primary school at Easton in just three months' time. During the summer holidays two mobile classrooms and two sets of mobile toilets arrived on our site along with a large removal van full of equipment and furniture from Honingham Primary.

On the first day of the autumn term the first children from Honingham School arrived in their new blue school uniforms to the newly designated St

Peter's Church of England Voluntary Controlled Primary School. We had an extra teacher in Mr Evans who taught all the junior children in a 'mobile' and we had more classroom and break-time support staff.

The architects from the County Council brought the plans for the new building (which would join on to the old one) to a governors' meeting with some trepidation. It was a completely innovative and 'different' building with curved steel roofs. They thought that village school governors would be conservative and dislike the plans – they were wrong. The governors were most enthusiastic.

For the next few months we lived with building work going on around us. It was an exciting time, especially as the builders let the pupils see as much as was safely possible. We buried a time capsule in the foundations. We even had an OFSTED inspection when the new building was nearly complete.

We moved into the new building in September 1997 with new furniture and equipment. We now had four classrooms, two offices, a large all-purpose hall, new toilets and a staff room. It was a building to be proud of, officially opened by the Bishop of Lynn in November 1997. I enjoyed showing numerous visitors around, including County Council architects from all over England.

It was an exciting time, during which the school roll continued to grow to nearly 100, but we never lost the sense of a small community and enjoyed good links with Easton and the surrounding villages, with St Peter's Church, Easton College and other schools in the area. There was always a keen band of parents who organised fairs, social evenings, extra treats for the children and generally supported the school in every way; and dedicated, hard-working staff and governors.

The school is set to develop and grow further under the leadership of Mrs Christine Livings as the village continues to expand.

A Typical Day at St Peter's

by Bethany and Megan Simmons, aged ten and eight, 20.12.2003

The school gates open at 8.45a.m. and the children are allowed into the class at 8.50a.m. The register is called between 9 and 9.10a.m. We do early work, this is usually a problem to solve. The first lesson is normally maths and lasts for an hour. We then have assembly, this is sometimes taken by the Revd Angela. We then have a drink and biscuits and then go outside to play. Literacy is normally our second lesson and ends at noon. Lunch is served in the hall, you may bring in a packed lunch or have a cooked meal which is brought into the school. Once we have finished we can go out to play – football, skipping or ball games. The first lesson of the afternoon is reading, and subjects also covered are IT computer work, DT, art and design, geography, science, PE and swimming. School finishes at 3.15p.m.

Above: *The reception class in the New School, 1998.*

Left: *Christmas Group 1999/2000.*

Below: *Group of children outside the New School, 1998/99.*

Left: *Five shepherds in the nativity play.*

Below: *A group at the school gates.*

Bottom: *View of the New School with its extension, 1999.*

Below: *Party time, 1999/2000.*

Left: *New Village School before the extension, 1974.*

Top left: *Cookery class, 1996/97.*
Above: *The school gym, c.1990s.*

Above: *Making a snowman in the playground, 1985.*
Below: *Children who were presented with swimming certificates, 1996.*

A class with Mrs Pease in 1983 (above) *and another class* (below) *with Mrs Pease on the left and Mrs Courtney.*

The Old School as it is now; it is a private house.

Staff and pupils at Easton School, 2004. Left to right, back row: *Kate Carter (teacher), Catherine Ross (teacher), Sonia Lawn (secretary), Rebecca Newman (teacher, assistant head), Margaret Seely (teaching assistant), Linda Ford (teacher), Carole Mortimer (teaching assistant);* front row: *Barry Millard (caretaker), Georgia Middleton (Class 1, age five), Amy Sharman (Class 3, age nine), Max Farqhar (Class 4, age nine), Sam Naylor (Class 4, age nine), Christine Livings (head teacher).*

Chapter Six

Easton College

Nestling in the hollow between the village of Easton and the River Yare is Easton Hall, which for many years was the principal's house for Easton College. You could easily miss the 1950s and '60s buildings tucked away amongst the trees, but the college is now more noticeable with its buildings for the new millennium standing out on higher ground.

In total the college has about 285 hectares (700 acres) of land which was purchased by Norfolk County Council in 1949 as a permanent home for residential agricultural education. It was officially opened by Lord Carrington in 1953, although its first students came in 1951. Initially the students boarded at Wymondham College and were brought to Easton by bus, but then hostels were built at the college along with many of the facilities apparent in 2004.

The first principal was Mr W.J. Garnett and, together with some of the early staff, he is remembered in the road names for the new housing development in Easton opposite the dairy buildings; this land was sold by the college to finance its new building programme and the jubilee building was completed in 2003.

Remembering the first staff in this way was the idea of Heriot Cossey, who still lives in Easton and was himself one of the first students at the college. In its early days the college was known as the Norfolk School of Agriculture, and the principal's slogan was 'four hundred not forty', referring to the growth in numbers of the residential students as he was not a great believer in part-time education. By 1965 the college could accommodate 80 full-time students and 100 by 1970.

In 1974 Mr Garnett was succeeded by David Crowe and later that year, following the national trend, the college became the Norfolk College of Agriculture and Horticulture. With part-time agricultural education based at Easton there was considerable development which resulted in mobile classrooms, as new courses including horticulture and the new youth training scheme produced a great surge of students finding their way to Easton, increasingly by car! Courses in conservation and countryside management, floristry and arboriculture competed for resources with the traditional agriculture and horticulture, and in 1991 the name of the establishment was changed to Easton College to reflect these trends.

By this time David Crowe had retired and in 1987 Ted Preston became the first principal to live off site. The days of blazers for high tea and lights out at 10.30p.m. or even earlier were long gone. There were

big plans to bring the police on to the Easton site to share facilities. New teaching accommodation surrounding Easton Hall was planned, and furniture was ordered, but all of this came to nothing and the hall became known as the White House – the administration centre. More mobile classrooms and some glass houses also sprang up, as the old established Burlingham Horticultural site near Acle was unceremoniously closed and eventually sold.

Always strapped for cash, the future of the college looked brighter when, almost overnight, in 1993 the Government took further education out of County Council control and proposed direct funding. It took some time to get the sums anywhere near right, during which time courses in equine studies and animal care (pets) came on to the scene. A surprise change of principal saw David Lawrence in the hot seat and Easton, unlike many similar colleges, avoided merging with larger establishments and has remained independent.

The ability to sell land has undoubtedly helped facilitate the most recent developments and it is a tribute to all the former staff and students that they achieved so much with so little. Many of the staff, particularly on the farm and the domestic front, were and still are from established Easton families who have managed to keep the spirit of Easton College alive through some pretty dark days. In 1987 the *Eastern Daily Press* announced that there were plans to close it!

At the time of writing, a massive sports hall, student services and teaching complex dominates the skyline with its red cladding; a far cry from its predecessor, an Atcost Barn with sides. This building which straddled the millennium, heralded the development of sports and public-services courses and Easton Gym Club (the one village organisation to use the college facilities regularly), but they have all but outgrown what the college can offer.

A new blue-coloured teaching and learning resources centre, known as the Jubilee Building, is the latest addition and at the time of writing is undergoing some horticultural softening of the landscape. This has come at a time when agriculture is in a difficult economic state. The college farm, which once employed a series of real characters as farm managers, with a large staff who passed their skills on to the students, is now largely managed by Morley Research Centre. Easton College has become the College in the Countryside and reflects diversification in the widest possible sense since its small beginnings 50 years ago.

Easton College's main building, 1960s.

Group of students and staff at Easton College, mid-1970s. The staff in the second row are, left to right:
Colin Cram, Melvyn Nelson, Ron Leadenham, Geoff Cox, Peter Metcalf and Les Plane; front row:
*Gordon Reynolds, Peter Underdown, Tony Dingle, Anthony Eddington, Joan Priest (housekeeper),
David Crowe (principal), Bill Wheeler (vice-principal), Harold Segger, John Paine,
Ivor Watkins and Bridget Eagle.*

Harvesting the hay, 1950s.

A college open day, early 1950s, with Bob Harrowven driving the front tractor and Anthony Eddington sitting at the back. Bill Wheeler is on the second tractor.

Below: *The college sign showing St Walstan, the patron saint of agricultural workers, who died in 1016. A very humble man with healing powers for humans and animals, it is said that wherever the oxen cart carrying his body for burial at Bawburgh stopped, a spring sprang up. The shield on the sign represents the four-course rotation of turnips, barley, wheat and clover.*

NORFOLK EDUCATION COMMITTEE

NORFOLK SCHOOL OF AGRICULTURE

Official Opening

BY

The Rt. Hon. SIR THOMAS DUGDALE, Bt., T.D., M.P.
Minister of Agriculture

ON

FRIDAY
30th OCTOBER, 1953
at 3 p.m.

Souvenir Programme

Above: *The White House – now used as offices.*

Left: *Programme of the official opening of the college, 30 October 1953.*

Below: *The domestic staff, c.1980s. Left to right: June Shingles, Hilda Watts, Ruby McCadden, Chrissie Mortimer and Heather Goldsmith.*

Right: *Geoff Quilter, the pig man at Easton College, late 1950s or early 1960s.*

Below: *Billy Thorne received a long-service award for working at the college for 40 years. He retired in 1971.*

Below: *Mr Crowe presenting leaving gifts to,* left to right, top: *Anthony Eddington, Peter Underdown;* centre: *Margaret Ince;* bottom: *Geoff Quilter and Les Plane.*

Bottom: *The Marlingford herd at Easton College, late 1960s.*

Right: *Geoff Quilter, the pig man at Easton College, late 1950s or early 1960s.*

Above: *Aerial photograph of Easton College, 1990s.*

Bottom: *The Duchess of Kent at Easton College, 5 July 1978.*

Memories of Easton College

by Hazel Harrowven

I worked for 31 years at the college in the dining-room and saw many changes. There have been four principals, Mr Garnett being the first one and the present principal [2004] is Mr Lawrence. I enjoyed my work and met lots of people in television and radio who used to visit the college. The late Ted Ellis was a regular visitor for tea in Miss Bomber's time, as well as David Richardson and Bernard Matthews to name but a few. Our highlight was when the Duchess of Kent came – she was a very gracious lady and there was such excitement, the place swarming with police

and dogs and us ladies decked out in our new uniforms which the Duchess did comment on, saying how nice we looked. I served her with afternoon tea.

We had conferences during the year, some of them international, with young people from all over the world. It was long hours but enjoyable and I often did not arrive home until midnight. The prize-giving was a huge affair and we worked from seven in the morning on preparing the sandwiches and laying the tables. Some 300 people came into the dining-room to enjoy a very good afternoon tea, and our chefs excelled themselves with cakes and pastries.

We had concerts in the hall (old hall) with the staff entertaining us, Mr Crowe with his monologues and Mr Gordon Reynolds with his Dame Edna routine. We came out with our sides aching from laughter. At Christmas there was carol singing round the tree in the front hall with coffee and mince pies.

At the Royal Norfolk Show we served teas in the college tent, working in shifts on the two days of the show. Over the years I saw lots of the royal family while I worked there, it was really authentic with the cows mooing in the tent next to us. We also looked after the military at the college who were at the show for the two days parading in the grand ring.

I have only happy memories of the college, good staff and working in beautiful surroundings.

Chapter Seven

Businesses

Village Post Office

The first Post Office was in the Loke by the side of the school and comprised two cottages knocked into one. It was reputedly run by Mrs Libby Blythe and then her son Mr Percy Blythe, who in 1947 moved with his family to the bungalow adjoining the hair-dressing salon on Marlingford Road as it is now. A Post Office was then opened in the back room of the bungalow. It consisted of a long wooden counter and a couple of chairs; there was no glass partition in those days. Mr Blythe ran this until the bungalow was extended into a small general store. His daughter Leslie and son in-law Ian Deeks then ran it and the Post Office was transferred into the shop. Over the years it has changed hands a number of times, at first being taken on by Peter and Audrey Foster, then June and Fred Marsh. The last people to run it were Dave and Sue Cooper, during whose time there was a hold-up! Raiders armed with a sawn-off shotgun and a knife terrified Sue and the cus-tomers. Soon after the couple closed the shop but kept the Post Office open – from 1994 this was run by Beryl Hillsden.

Postman Bob Ponder during the 1960s.

Beryl retired on 24 April 2001 when Easton Post Office closed for the last time, having provided not only a good service for its cus-tomers, but also an ideal meeting place where people tended to stop for a chat. The church decided to start a drop-in on a Tuesday morning at the Village Hall to keep a contact going for the parishioners, and the Car Community Scheme was set up to help people get their pensions.

During Beryl's time in the Post Office she was burgled. It was a terrible ordeal for her as the two young boys wore balaclavas and were armed with a gun, but she bravely opened up the next morning. Sadly, however, the shock proved too much for her, affecting her nerves so that she couldn't sleep. She subsequently became ill and carried on the Post Office as best she could, but in the end she had to retire. At her retirement party she said that people had been so kind and that she felt very sad that she had to leave. She had greatly enjoyed being the postmistress.

At the Parish Council meeting in March 2001 we were advised that our Post Office would close on Tuesday 24 April. A steering group headed by Revd Angela Reynolds was formed to explore a way of reopening the facility. We were aware that the Department of Trade and Industry had proposals in hand to help Post Offices in rural areas by means of a new grant scheme, but exact details had not been agreed and signed. We held regular monthly meetings with Post Watch and Post Office represen-tatives at the 'Pop-In' as we had a to find suitable premises and someone to run the Post Office. We also applied to South Norfolk Council and Vital Villages for details of their grant schemes. Later in the year we learned that Mr Maurice Houldsworth, a sub-postmaster at Costessey, had expressed an interest in running a part-time sub-Post Office for us, and details of the Post Office Start-up Scheme were made available. As no suitable premises had been found we contacted the Village Hall regarding the possibility of building an exten-sion. Jack Curl, a parish councillor, drew up plans and, after consultations with both South Norfolk Council and the Post Office, costings were obtained. Brenda Daynes, vice-chairman of the Parish Council, and Wendy Dorr completed the forms to apply for grants from the Post Office, Vital Villages and South Norfolk Council to cover the cost of the building and fitting out the interior. We were successful in obtaining these grants and Michael Sparkes of Building Services Easton began work in September 2002.

The new part-time sub-Post Office opened on Tuesday 5 November 2002 at 9a.m. Radio Norfolk broadcast an interview with Brenda Daynes and Maurice Houldsworth and the *Evening News* pub-lished a photo and details of the opening. Revd Angela Reynolds prayed for the new building to an audience and parishioners, with Brenda Daynes and Wendy Dorr cutting the ribbon to declare the Post Office open. We then had refreshments in the Village Hall for the representatives from the Post Office, Vital Villages, South Norfolk Council and Easton Parish Council. These were provided by the 'Pop-In' and Anne Dunbar made a cake decorated in Post Office colours. Stephen Dorrington, Norfolk County Councillor, took photographs of the event. At the time of writing the Post Office has been running for over a year and has been a great success.

❧ Easton Post Office ❧

Left: *Beryl Hillsden (right) at her farewell party, the day she retired from the Post Office, 2001.*

Right: *Mr Houldsworth at Easton Post Office, 2002.*

Right: *Cheerful local postie Colin Atkins is married with two little boys, 2003.*

Left: *Inside the old Post Office, 2001.*

The old Post Office on the day that it shut, 2001.

The Dog

The last sign at The Dog.

The pub stands on the old A47 and was built in 1611 as a coaching inn which provided refreshment to the many travellers between Norwich and King's Lynn. The first dated records are from 1845 when The Dog was kept by Henry Buxton and horse-drawn coaches were still stopping here on their journeys. The earliest photograph of the inn dates from c.1900.

The authors received a letter from Mr Watling of Southminster in Essex who had traced his family back to Easton in the year 1811. The letter states that his family history is interwoven between Easton and Marlingford. A Charles Watling was born at Marlingford to John and Ann Watling in about 1811. He married Ann Moor in 1834 at Marlingford, and they had a son John, who was born in 1841 at Easton, but Ann died in 1846 (her death being attributed in records to 'decay'!). In 1847 Charles married Harriet Payne, the sister of his brother John's wife Matilda (whose grave is the first on the right inside Easton churchyard gate). In 1849 another boy, William, was born to Charles and Harriet. Charles died of injuries in 1850 following a brawl outside The Dog (he is recorded as having been 'feloniously killed and slayed'). Harriet died in 1853 at Easton with the fever, followed by the death of their second child, William, at the age of six, with convulsions.

The following excerpts are taken from the *Norfolk Chronicle* and *Norwich Gazette* dated 6 July 1850:

MANSLAUGHTER

On Monday an inquest was held at the "Dog Inn" Easton before Mr Pilgrim, one of the County Coroners, on the body of Charles Watling of Easton, whose death had been occasioned by severe blows afflicted upon him by William Stone of the same parish. It appears that the deceased and Stone were both Labourers in Easton. On the night of Tuesday week, Watling was in the "Dog" and was drinking his beer, Stone came in, Watling asked him to take a glass of which Stone replied "No I am not going to drink with such a b----- fellow as you", Stone afterwards went out and two other men who had also been in the public house left to go home.

Whilst they were standing on the corner of the road Watling came out and passed them, they heard Stone say something and after some words had passed, he added "I'll give you a bang on the head if you don't take the law of me". Watling replied "There shall be no law but that of our own making".

Stone stripped to fight, but Watling did not follow his example, Stone ran up and caught Watling by the hips and Watling caught Stone by the collar. In the first fall Watling was on top of his opponent, a man of the name of Thorald pulled him over. Stone got up whilst Watling was on the ground and kicked him most violently in the lower part of his body, having on at the time thick shoes plated with iron.

All the parties appear then to have separated and Watling being left behind crawled home.

The injuries the poor fellow had received appear to have been of a frightful and fatal description, for after lingering in great pain he died on Sunday afternoon.

He leaves a wife and three children, Stone is also a married man.

The jury of which J.H. Gurney Esq. was foreman, was a most respectable one, the case was only part heard on Monday and stands adjourned to today (Friday). Stone is in custody.

Saturday 13 July 1850 saw this report in the papers:

On Friday last Mr Pilgrim held and adjourned inquest at the "Dog Inn" Easton, on the body of Charles Watling, labourer of that parish, who died of wounds inflicted in a barbarous manner, by another labourer, named William Stone.

The particulars of this case have already been published and they're being no doubt as to the facts it is unnecessary to give the depositions at length.

On Friday evidence was given in information of previous statements showing the most brutal and barbarous manner in which the deceased had been treated and exhibiting a degree of ferocity on the part of Stone that would have been seen as disgraceful to savages.

After all the witnesses had been examined, Mr Pilgrim explained to the jury the difference between murder and manslaughter, and he referred to several cases, he expressed his satisfaction at seeing so respectable a jury assembled, feeling assured from the attention they had given to the case, they would come to a proper conclusion.

After consulting for more than half an hour, the jury returned a verdict of manslaughter against William Stone and recorded their opinion that John Maddis, Elijah Johnson and James Hurrell were greatly to blame for not endeavouring to prevent the melancholy catastrophe.

LICENSEES OF THE DOG

Henry Buxton	1836–56
aged 44 in 1851 and farmer of 50 acres	
Mary Buxton	1861–75
aged 59 in 1861 and farmer of 94 acres	
Andrew Penman	1879–81
and farmer of 96 acres in 1881	
Isaac and Richard Budden	1883
Walter Howard Randall	1888–96
Walter Bridges	1900
John Robert Bridges	1904–08
Robert John Bridges	1912
Mrs Eliza Bridges	1916
Harry J. Mann	1922
Gordon Edward Greenwood	1925–29
Herbert Sidney Tuck	1933–37
Mr Earl	1962

The Dog in the late 1940s.

The Dog in the 1950s.

The Dog in the 1930s.

The pub looking in the direction of the church. The cottages you see were pulled down when the road was straightened. Note the road with no pavements in this view from the late-nineteenth century.

Above and below: *The Des Amis Restaurant, c.2001.*

Above: *Denis Rosembert at the Des Amis Restaurant, c.2000.*

Above: *Leslie Tuck in RAF uniform when he was a navigator, 1940s.*

Below: *Leslie Tuck in 1937.*

Right: *The Dog with outhouses and the barn, 1963.*

Bikers gathered outside The Dog, c.1990s.

The following was published on 3 August at the Crown Court:

Mr Justice Patterson took the seat.
William Stone (age 27) was charged with having at Easton killed and slain one Charles Watling of that parish. The prisoner pleaded guilty and his Lordship, after having commented on the enormity of the offence, sentenced him to ten years transportation.

On 24 August the following was noted in relation to the 'removal of convicts': 'The following transports were on Wednesday morning removed from Norwich Castle by the Governor of Wakefield Prison. William Stone plus others.' In the census subsequent to Stone's transportation, it was shown that his wife and children were living with her brother and his family.

In 1922 the local brewery was Bullards and the publican at The Dog was Harry Mann. He had ten children, all of whom are thought to have survived into adulthood. In those days there was a barn at the back of the pub, which housed a carrier's cart and the local villagers could hire this vehicle to go to Norwich and back. The grooms included Messrs Hipkin, Greenwood and Reeve.

During the 1930s and '40s the men of the village played football in the field at the back of the pub, which in those days was a meeting-place for men and women alike. They had special events there and one of them was on VJ Day when they celebrated with a party and bonfire on the car park, which in those days was just earth. They were supplied with beer by Mr Tuck and cooked potatoes in the hot ashes.

The pub at this time consisted of a smoke room, main bar and lounge, and was heated by coal fires. Darts and cards were played. The landlord Bert Tuck (who also farmed the land

Right: *Ken Watling, who provided the authors with information about the murder at The Dog, c.1990s.*

The grave of Matilda Watling in the churchyard.

and kept pigs, chickens and cows) and his wife Nellie had two children, Ann and Leslie. Leslie joined the Airforce in 1943 as a navigator. He did his training in Canada and qualified in July 1944. He lived in the house behind the Old School but sadly, while we were writing this book, he died (on 20 November 2003).

Bertie Sparkes said that during the war two RAF Lancaster bombers flew low over the school 'dipping their wings', which was all very exciting for the children. It transpired that in each of the planes the two navigators were known to the villagers, one being Les Tuck and the other Freddie Fox's brother.

The publicans in the 1940s–'50s were Mr Tuck and then Mr Earl. When Bert ran The Dog, the barn, which had by this time been made into a sort of Village Hall with parquet flooring, was used for parties and local dances. Marge Hawes and her mother supplied the music; they played the dulcimer and piano. The man who organised these events was Donny Mortimer. Bob Ponder said that he remembered when Donny brought a kipper into the pub one day and cooked it on the fire, which didn't please Annie Tuck at all (one can imagine the smell). Outside the pub there was a chain-link fence, which was used by the local children as a swing. The children were also experts at scrumping, taking apples from the tree in the corner of the bowling-green, and pinching turnips from the garden and eating them raw. They said they were never caught.

During the war the pub was a very busy place. The villagers remember that so many people, including many men from the Forces (stationed at the both English and American bases), drank there that it was not unusual for the drink to run out by Wednesday. It is thought that the American pilots used The Dog as a marker when coming into land!

During the time when Mr Earl had the pub a fishmonger sold cockles and mussels on Saturday nights outside on the car park.

The barn at the back of the pub was used in the late 1950s to house the tractor and farm equipment. It eventually fell down in about 1963 and the site has since been built upon. Also beside the barn was a shed where local people left their bikes to catch the bus into Norwich; it was always full.

The pub has now become a restaurant called Des Amis, owned by Mr Denis Rosembert, who lives above with his wife Dinah, two daughters Denise and Kersha, and a son, Dean. It was opened in 1997 and specialises in French Creole and Cajun food. The last extension in 2002 was to build accommodation once again for the traveller. The Rosemberts have, however, left the old listed wall in the front as this dates back to the 1700s.

John Pratt, 1920s–'30s

John Pratt owned the local shop and bungalow (actually a railway carriage) on the corner of Bawburgh Lane (Bawburgh Road) and Dereham Road. A slaughterhouse was attached and each month he slaughtered about 100 pigs, assisted by his brother Ernie. These pigs were collected in two vehicles and taken to London for distribution. At the same time he delivered pork to local butchers and sold home-made pork sausages from a van which he drove himself. During the war relations who got bombed out in Norwich lived in the slaughterhouse. Meanwhile, Bessie, John's wife, made and sold pork cheeses at 4d. each and ran the general store. John was, for a time, part-time chauffeur for Mr Morse at Costessey Lodge on the old A47 and on occasions he also helped Billy Dade as a plasterer. At weekends Bessie made ice-cream in the slaughterhouse (she had a secret recipe). Can you imagine this being done today? The ice-cream was sold on Saturday nights at local dances and on Sunday afternoons at the Costessey fields at the top of Gurney Road (before the area was developed). John and Bessie and their family moved to Costessey in 1936. The shop was taken over by Miss Violet Buck in the 1940s.

Below: *The shop owned by Mr and Mrs Pratt who are shown here* (right) *in the 1930s.*

Bob Buck

Hilda Peacock fondly remembers Buck's shop:

As a little-un I loved going up the steps into his strange little building with its medley of smells – oil, candles, sweets, etc. – and gazing at the big jars of sweets, especially the one with the Smarties in. This jar never seemed to empty but the colours of the sweets became progressively paler. Bob lived with his old Aunt Violet and would appear from the side of the shop like some character from a Dickens novel – complete with a sniff! It was sad when they both passed away and the old shop and bungalow were pulled down.

Pauline Parsons remembers a lovely yellow duster which was hanging up, for sale, and as the years went by it got blacker and blacker. Mr Buck died at the back of the shop, possibly from hypothermia.

Gypsy Families

Before and during the war a gypsy family called Lamb parked on the Pytle (plot of ground) on the corner of Norwich Road (Dereham Road) and Bawburgh Lane, opposite Pratt's shop. Another gypsy family named Grey frequently visited them. Both families made umbrellas and pegs in large quantities, plus other small items.

🌿 The Rembrandt 🌿

Left: *Christmas at The Rembrandt, 1970s.*

Below: *Lucia and Chris, owners of the fish and chip shop, pictured at The Rembrandt, 2003.*

Bottom: *Groups outside the fish and chip shop gathered for the 2003 village calendar. Left to right: Local postman, paperboys and girls, a group from the Bowls Club, the AA man, fish and chip waiters and waitresses, and the Judo Club, 2002.*

Chef Riccobena, owner of The Rembrandt, 1977.

Charlie Hart

Charlie Hart had an electrical business. He built his own house called Highview in the early 1920s. It was a very early prefabricated building, which has since been bricked around, and is the house next to the Vicarage. He ran the electrical store from the top floor, using a wooden staircase outside the house. This is where we bought our light bulbs and had the accumulators charged during the war. In the large garage beside the house he had a charabanc, which he used for school runs and outings, or for private hire, in the 1920s and '30s. He was a school manager, churchwarden and chorister, and also a member of the Easton Bowls Club. During the war he was a member of the ARP. Mrs Hart was headmistress at Easton from 1921–26 and also ran the first-aid post in the village during the war. Villagers also paid their hospital contributions to her for years (this was a sort of insurance in case of hospitalisation and if money was required for glasses, etc.). Charlie had one of the first cars and telephones before the war and was a well-respected person.

Bakery, The Rembrandt & The Fish and Chip Shop

The premises were originally built as a bakery, in the centre of the village, in c.1938. The first occupant and owner was Mr Alfred Cooper, who ran the bakery and delivered by van to surrounding villages. There was a small shop and Dolly Harrowven worked there after leaving school, selling the bread. In the mid-1940s the bakery was taken over by Mr and Mrs Chapman. In the 1950s it changed hands again to Mr and Mrs John Kitchen who opened a bigger bakery and also had a bread round. Next to occupy the premises was a young man who was born and brought up in Easton, Jim Ponder, who converted it into a large grocery shop selling a variety of goods, and the old bakehouse was turned into a café. Jim also owned the garage on the opposite side of the road for several years.

In 1963 a new owner, Mr Michael Hubbard, took over the premises and, together with Wiskard Builders, made a great deal of alterations. A large beamed and panelled restaurant took shape, with a bungalow also built at the back for living accommodation. The local tradesmen employed included Neville Bird, a professional carpenter. It was opened as a first-class restaurant in 1965 and was named 'The Rembrandt'. Michael and Maria Hubbard ran the business. Maria was a very good chef and did the cooking, including a variety of German dishes, and their daughter Michelle waited on tables. As trade increased more help was needed and a local girl, June Bird, was employed. She continued to work there for six years. The Rembrandt had another owner in January 1975 when Bruno Riccobena arrived. He was born a cockney with an Italian father and was an excellent chef, soon building up trade. His regular customers came from miles away each week to sample his speciality dishes. In 1977 he was awarded one of the highest accolades in the world of French Cuisine, 'The Maitise Escoffier', for which the Association Culinaire Francaise presented him with a gold medal and diploma. He was a West End chef for many years, where he trained at the Dorchester, and was also head chef at the Connaught Rooms and Pickwick Club. For ten years he was executive chef and catering adviser to the BBC's film units, travelling all over Europe with them. He also received many other awards before coming to Easton. The Rembrandt got very busy, especially at weekends when four waitresses were needed to cope. By this time June was head waitress, in charge of the restaurant, and on special days such as Mothering Sunday and Easter Day it would be double booked with more than 100 customers. Christmas Eve was another busy session and customers never wanted to leave, but tables had to be set for the next day before staff could have their Christmas party. The staff left in the early hours to be back at 9a.m. for a very hectic Christmas day and were expected to stay for a meal with the Riccobena family when all was cleared up.

Again Bruno was an exceptional man, very kind and thoughtful, full of fun which made it a very happy place to work. It was a great loss when he died suddenly in 1989 – we lost a great friend. Pat Wiepen worked alongside him in his kitchen for 15 years. June also worked for Bruno for 15 years (21 years altogether at The Rembrandt). Two other people owned the restaurant for short periods and the present owners run a successful restaurant at the time of writing.

In 2004 the premises are used as a fish and chip shop, run by the Motta family. Mauro (Mal) and Rose, with their three children, Lucia, Christian and Dario, took over The Rembrandt in 1991 and ran it as a takeaway and restaurant. This is a very successful enterprise serving fresh fish in pleasant surroundings and employing many local young people, providing friendly service and football news from Mal. In 2001 the business was passed on to Lucia, the daughter, and, with her partner Chris (Skip) and son Davide, she continues to serve the best fish meals in the traditional way.

The Rembrandt.

Building Services (Easton) Ltd

Michael Sparkes, Fred Betts and Bertie Sparkes, 1980s.

Fred Betts and Bert Sparkes started the business in the 1950s, when Fred (aged 26 at the time) was a bricklayer and Bert (24) a carpenter. They started with £50, a motorbike and sidecar and an old butcher's van. Some of their equipment was made in Bert's parents' greenhouse, and the office was an old chicken house in the same garden. As time went on they bought part of the garden from Bert's parents, along with part of Fred and Doris Fox's garden, to form a builder's yard, where the business remains in 2004. The business in those days was called Betts & Sparkes Ltd, Building Services (Easton) Ltd being started at a later date. Both businesses were operated together until Fred left in 1982. At this point Betts & Sparkes Ltd was discontinued and Building Services (Easton) Ltd was then expanded.

The company has been a great employer of local men and have worked for councils, the diocese, the fire service, National Trust, Royal Norfolk Agricultural Association, Bullards Brewery (on the recommendation of the late Leslie Tuck who was a surveyor for Bullards Brewery) and Norfolk College of Agriculture, as well as many private individuals. Many of Fred and Bert's relatives have worked for the firm – Michael Sparkes, Bert's son, did an apprenticeship with Riley Builders on leaving school, and after that started with Bert in 1982. In 1994, on reaching official retirement age, Bert gradually took a back seat, in semi-retirement, with a view to a well-earned full retirement, but even in 2004 Bert has not yet fully retired. The firm is still very busy after 50 years of business and Michael Sparkes is carrying on the business in much the same way as his father before him, with some minor changes, of course. Neil Middleton started as a bricklayer apprentice with the firm on leaving school in 1963 and is still a member of staff in 2004. The business retains the same good name, which is justly earned by all concerned.

Right: *Sid Sparkes (born 1892), a Corporal in the Cold Stream Guards during the First World War (seen here c.1914), was the only survivor of his regiment. He was honoured by working as a guard at Buckingham Palace for two weeks.*

Adam's Automotive Engineering

Adam Pointer grew up heavily involved with veteran and classic cars, not forgetting old lawnmowers. On leaving school in 1980 he took an apprenticeship with a plant-hire firm formerly known as Heyhoe Bros near Salhouse. This enabled him to pursue his passion not only for cars, but everything mechanical from cement mixers to bulldozers. Then, in 1989 Adam had an opportunity to buy his own premises, the site which had previously been used by the coachworks at Easton, which was already a building steeped in history. The history of the site goes back to the nineteenth century, when it had had two blacksmiths' forges and its own water-supply, and was a coaching stop between Norwich and King's Lynn. Its purpose was to repair all manner of horse-drawn vehicles, employing various residents of Easton. This had always been used as a vehicular works so, on discovering its history, Adam jumped at the chance to buy it. Adam started his own business importing British classic cars from America, which were then stored and sold at the premises. When the business started to pick up his father-in-law Eric Fitchurch (who had worked at Lola racing cars of Huntingdon) joined him. Together they restored and maintained classic, veteran and vintage cars, and as a pair of classic-car-rally enthusiasts they entered into numerous events across Europe, including the Monte Carlo Challenge, in which they became team winners two years in succession.

The business then expanded into preparing classic rally cars for competitions, serving many customers from afar as Japan to our Home Counties, taking many customers to numerous successes. Andrew Kitchen joined the business in 1998 to assist with the running of the garage and help the two workmen, Eric Fitzhugh and Adam Pointer, cope with demand. Apart from restoring cars the business is set up to repair and restore obsolete parts and export them to many places, such as Israel, Ireland and mainland Europe.

Easton Woodworks

Mr Hogg bought the carpenter's shop and land from Mr Brand in about 1946. He was an accomplished wood turner who soon outgrew the workshop and had a much larger factory built back from the road. He always helped local people, providing kindling for their fires from his left-over wood. He employed many village lads, one being Doug Harrowven who started work straight from school, in 1956. The first things he remembers making were wooden fruit bowls, stair-rods, chair legs, rolling-pins and duffle-coat buttons – anything that could be turned on a lathe. Mr Hogg worked in the yard for 55 years.

Other Businesses

The hairdressers in the old Post Office is owned and run by Jenny Rowley, with stylist Jane Connolly. The company started on 2 May 2001, but for many years previously they worked at Barnham Broom Hotel.

Mr Harold Eastoe was a furniture restorer in the 1930s. Mr Fred Fincham had a dairy on the Norwich Road in the 1930s.

Chapter Eight

Easton at Leisure

Parish councils came into being by an Act of Parliament in 1894. The first Parish Council meeting at Easton took place on 4 February 1895 in the Old School. Present at that first meeting were Mr H. Harrowven, Mr T. Harrowven, Mr A. Hook, Mr W. Middleton and Mr H. Stone. The first chairman was a Mr Frederick Vincent Cole of Marlingford, the vice-chairman was Mr W. Middleton and the parish clerk was Mr Clark of Easton. In the records office we have found the first minute book which holds records from 1895–1912. The only other books are from 1954 to the present day.

From the minute book of May 1960 it can be seen that the Parish Council had grown to seven members – Mr Leckenby (chairman), Mr H.S. Roberson, Mr V. Brand, Mr C.J. Sweet, Mr C.H. Barnard, Mr C.L. Addis and Mr A. Simkin.

In 2004 the Parish Council consists of seven parishioners, and they would normally be in office for a three-year period. Back in May 1961 we had 13 applications of names to be put forward. This meant that we had to have an election and the successful candidates were Revd H.W. Paine, Mr C. Earl, Mr A.G. Wales, Mrs M.I. Eddington, Mr A. Simkin, Mr B.L. Sparkes and Mr S.A. Peacock. In those days we were part of the Forehoe and Henstead Rural District Council. As from 1969 the council meetings were held in the new village hall.

One of the well-known chairmen was Mr Percy Buxton, who was co-opted on to the Parish Council in November 1972. He was chairman from May 1974–80, and retired from the council in January 1982.

Mr Peacock, who became chairman of the Parish Council and also served on the South Norfolk District Council, retired in May 1983 after 22 years. The village had a collection in recognition of his many years of voluntary service and presented him with a set of bowls.

During 1973 two places became vacant on the Parish Council and six names were put forward, resulting in an election. This is when Mrs Angela Reynolds (now the vicar) and Mr David Ditton were elected.

Mr Ditton became chairman in 1983 and remained in this post until 1991. The Norfolk Association of Parish and Town Councils have a ballot each year for a Parish Council chairman to attend the Buckingham Palace Garden Party. In 1990 Mr David Ditton and his wife Jean were lucky enough to be successful in the ballot and attended the Garden Party on 24 July.

In 1991 Mr Roger Pegg then became chairman,

until his tragic death after a heart attack while sailing at Hickling Broad on 6 July 1994.

The chairmen after this date and up until 2004 were: Mary Blathwayt (chairwoman), Mr Steven Hood, Mr Peter Pease, Mr David Ditton (who is again the chairman at the time of writing). There are several people on the Parish Council who have served for many years: Mr Heriot Cossey, Mr Peter Pease, Mr Fred Marsham, Mrs Brenda Daynes, Mrs Mary Blathwayt, Mr Percy Buxton and Mr Stanley Peacock. The clerks over the years have been: Miss Hilda Peacock, Mr Hobson-Frohock, Mrs Edna Dickens, Mr Milburn, Mrs Sandra Lock, Mrs Elizabeth Plummer and Mr John Witcombe (in 2004). Mr Mike Tomlinson had also represented Easton as a South Norfolk councillor for 20 years until he retired in 2003.

EⁱⁱR

The Lord Chamberlain is commanded by Her Majesty to invite

Mr and Mrs D.H.J. Ditton

to a Garden Party at Buckingham Palace on Tuesday, 24th July, 1990 from 4 to 6 p.m.

Morning Dress, Uniform or Lounge Suit

Left: *Parish Council invitation to the Queen's Garden Party.*

Below: *Dave Ditton presenting Ivy Marsh with the award for the best-kept garden, 2003.*

Below: *The Parish Council having a rest, c.1980s.*

John Howes Charity

By his will dated 28 November 1863 (proved at Norwich, 16 January 1864), John Howes gave to the:

... Vicar and Churchwardens of the Parish of Easton £200 in trust, to be invested and contrived upon a Government security and the dividends arising there-from to be applied in the purchase of coals, blankets or articles of clothing to be distributed amongst the aged poor of the said Parish at the discretion of the said Vicar and Churchwardens for the time being on the said 3rd day of February yearly.

In 1900 the charity stood at £8.2s.6d. but due to the lack of interest on the capital the charity was abandoned.

Easton Church Room

by Brenda Daynes

On Saturday 18 October 1986 I went to work as usual at my flower shop in Hethersett. Everything was normal until I received a telephone call from my son Kevin asking if I could return home to collect his group's PA equipment from the Church Room as it had just been demolished by a tanker. I arrived home, collected Kevin and, finding the road closed, asked the policeman if we could drive to the hall and retrieve the equipment – much to my surprise we were allowed through. We asked permission to enter the remains of the building; we had to crawl on hands and knees to find the amplifiers and speakers – it was very dark inside and we should have taken a torch. Eventually we located everything and got it all out. Kevin and his friends used the hall for rehearsing and had the instruments been set up the drums would have been almost at the point of impact. It was also lucky that a group of young boys who usually met there on Saturday mornings did not meet on this particular one. Kevin took some photographs of the damage whilst we were there; we were probably the first villagers to see it. The Church Room was insured but never replaced, the money going instead towards a new kitchen, toilet and upstairs room in the church.

There must be many people with memories of the Church Room, as it was the only meeting-place in the village at that time and an ideal location for wedding receptions, christenings and meetings, etc. I personally remember attending a Medau keep-fit class there, during which when you bounced balls clouds of dust rose from the floorboards and when swinging clubs we had to avoid the posts and the roof trusses, which was all good fun. The group of ladies in the photograph *(below)* were the Easton Medau Group who had just given a demonstration at the annual fête in the Vicarage grounds.

Above: *The tanker that crashed into the Church Room and demolished it, 1986.*

This image: *Keep-fit Medau class at the village fête in the Vicarage, 1970s. The back row includes: Pat Keats (instructor), Tottie Harrowven, Brenda Daynes, Brenda Nelson, Diane Ponder, Margie Hawes, Jean Fairweather; front row: Diane Frost, Mary Tuck, Helen Symonds, Sandra Coe.*

Village Halls

On 6 November 1926 Mr Colin Kidner of Easton Lodge wrote to Bullards & Son Ltd for permission to change the barn adjacent to The Dog into a village hall, the landlord of the pub at that time being Mr Greenwood. Mr Ernest Bullard gave permission, and proposed to spend about £100 on renovation. A good wooden dance floor was laid, two windows were put in, a panel door was installed facing the road, as also was a door at the other side, two tortoise stoves were fitted, the roof was repaired, the walls were distempered, and a pathway was made to The Dog for the use of the toilets. The rent was to be £10 per annum with Bullards paying the rates. There were two restrictions; any alcohol sold in the hall was to be bought from The Dog, and the other was that if the landlord required the hall for any purpose, the consent of the committee was not to be unreasonably withheld.

Later on the committee was given permission to erect a removable annex at the north side of the barn, which was to be taken away when the tenancy of the barn was given up. The hall was used for dances, the Men's Club, the WI, football meetings, etc. Every year there would be a Christmas treat for the children of the village – a Christmas party would be arranged and they would all be given a present.

The corrugated-tin Church Room dates back to 1919. The building was used for church meetings and events. In May 1933 the Revd Bracecampe wrote a letter to Captain J. Maine of West Lodge, secretary to the Village Hall committee, asking him why he had extended the Church Room. Captain Maine explained that the building was to be used to carry on the work of the church and also for other events. In November 1933 the committee gave notice to quit the Village Hall at The Dog and moved down to the Church Room (the Green Hut) and it was used as a Village Hall until a new hall was built in Marlingford Road, in 1968/9.

This has been used for almost 40 years by different organisations in the village, as well as for events such as fêtes, dances, social events, playgroup, etc. In 2004 there is a flourishing parent and toddler group, which meets every Wednesday, and the WI, Pop-In, Table Tennis Club, Parish Council and Good Companions all make use of the facility.

Above: The village fête, 1982 – at the front is Richard Harrowven.

Right: Left to right: Gloria Seaman, Gillian Cossey, Sheila Seaman and Dian Roberson in fancy dress for a village fête, 1950s.

New Village Hall and Recreation-Ground

When the Norwich southern bypass was planned in the 1980s it was obvious that the village of Easton was likely to grow once the main road no longer went through its centre. At this time it was realised that the existing Village Hall would become inadequate to meet the needs of the growing community and a search was started for a site on which to build a new one. As part of a planning agreement, a site on Dereham Road was made available to the village by a local landowner in 1996 and the Parish Council set up a steering committee to plan the project and to investigate methods of funding it. In July 1999 the present committee was formed and became a registered charity. After two questionnaires had been circulated, public meetings were held and a professional feasibility study was completed, plans were drawn up and the committee set about trying to raise money to fund the hall.

At the time of writing, two unsuccessful bids have been made to the Lottery Community Fund but a football pitch and car park have been established on the site. Fund-raising continues and the committee has been responsible for the organisation of the Easton Annual Village Quiz, two jumble sales a year, carol singing before Christmas, plus a variety of social events, with the intention of binding the community together whilst raising money for new and improved facilities. In 2003 Easton produced a village calendar with all the local organisations taking part and posing for photographs for each month of the year.

🌹 Church Room 🌹

Left: *Easton Youth Club in the Church Room. The two girls are Karen Harrowven and Sharon Carter, 1964.*

Below: Left to right: *Richard Harrowven, Daniel Jay, Christopher Hart and Judith Ditton at the 1978 fête.*

Below: *Medau keep-fit class, in the Village Hall, 2001.*

Below right: *Tea party in the old Church Room, early 1950s. Left to right: Trevor McCadden, Eric Peacock, Leslie Bailey, Ann Kidd, Andrew King.*

Background, below: *Village fête, 1979.*

Easton Women's Institute

Records show that as far back as 1927 or earlier, there was an active Women's Institute in Easton, of which Mrs Smith was the secretary. The ladies held their meetings in the Village Hall behind The Dog for several years, before the group was disbanded.

Then, in 1953, a group of women led by Mrs Coe of West Lodge, Lower Easton, decided to start up the Women's Institute again. The formation meeting took place on Thursday 12 March 1953 when 25 ladies met at the old Church Room on Dereham Road. A record of the first meeting of Easton Women's Institute on Thursday 26 March 1953 shows that a committee was formed of Mrs Stearn, Mrs Jolly, Mrs Coe, Mrs Greenacre, Mrs Garnett, Mrs Reid, Mrs Sweet, Mrs Bailey, Mrs Middleton and Mrs Knights. Mrs Elsie Coe was unanimously elected president.

Easton WI has a reputation for 'putting on a good spread' and often entertains visitors from the village and neighbouring Women's Institutes. Meetings are still held on the second Thursday of every month, generally in the Village Hall that was built in the 1960s. In August a coffee evening is held at a member's home. At the time of writing the WI has 27 members but has in the past had a membership of 44 and this has been as low as 14.

Easton WI has been a member of the Barford and District Group since 1959 and meetings are held in the spring and autumn every year, when members from Easton, Barford, Mattishall, Bowthorpe and Hethersett all join together in one of their meeting halls to enjoy a speaker and refreshments. There have also been joint celebrations for the millennium and the Queen's golden jubilee.

In the past some well-known people in the Norfolk Federation have been members of our WI, among them Mary Eddington, who was County vice-chairman, and Audrey Juby, who was County secretary for many years.

Above: *Women's Institute in the old Church Room (the Green Hut), 1976.*

Right: *The WI's 40th birthday party celebrated by past presidents, 1993. Left to right: Vera Barnard and Pam Hooker, Mary Blathwayt (current president), Margaret Cram, Mary Eddington and Linda Crowe.*

🌹 *Easton Women's Institute* 🌹

Left: *The WI won a prize for the best-dressed stall at the village fête in June 1989 held in the Vicarage grounds.*

Right: *Easton WI and what they do nowadays (2003)!*

Below: *Easton WI raised money for the Jenny Lind Hospital. Left to right: Ros Crowe and daughter Jemma, Margaret Seely and Son Timothy, early 1980s. The names of the nurses are not known.*

Below right: *Easton Women's Institute entered the Col Cater Cup competition at the Royal Norfolk Showground in 1994 and won 1st prize – Penny Howes is in the picture.*

Right: *A group of Easton Women's Institute members making flags for Queen Elizabeth II's silver jubilee in 1977.*

Good Companions

by Joan Chapman, Chairwoman

This club was started in May 1955 by the chairwoman Hilda Greenacre, the secretary Joan Ruddock and the remainder of the committee, which consisted of Mrs E. Greenacre, Mrs Ottaway, Mrs Knights, Mrs Walpole and Mrs Peacock. Nearly 50 years on it is still going strong. To begin with the meetings were held in the Church Room, on the corner of the Vicarage grounds – the only place which the village had at the time for such activities. The building was heated by means of a pot-bellied stove and oil stoves and a donation of 30 shillings was made to the Parochial Church Council for its use for a year; the main fund-raising activities were whist drives and jumble sales.

The following are notes taken from the club's minute books:

October 1957
It was decided to hold a jumble sale Saturday 2nd November and to have a grocery stall. After some discussion it was decided to hold a Whist drive on the 7th November and the 5th December, also have a draw. Mrs Ruddock was asked to procure 1 dozen books of 20 draw tickets. For prizes two members kindly said they would give a cake to the value of £1. Two others a 1lb box of chocolates. It was decided to buy a bottle of Port and Sherry out of Club Funds. The treasurer produced the balance sheet, which showed a balance of £39.2.11d.

Instead of the Christmas Party members were taken to the pantomime on the 30th January, a bus was booked from Semmence of Wymondham for £2.15.0d. Each member paid 2d. per meeting, this included a cup of tea and cake.

May 1960
The 5th Birthday Party on 18th May at 5.30p.m. was to be held. About twenty others to be invited. A birthday cake was ordered from Matthes, 5 dozen pastries and fancies. 2 dozen bridge rolls and 4 cut loaves from Smiths of Hethersett [they used to deliver bread to Easton]. Mrs Thorne and Mrs Peacock undertook to make the trifles. Mrs Walpole to cook meat. Gammon and salt beef to be purchased from Mr Blyth of Bawburgh. Mrs Ruddock and Mrs Sadd to make sausage rolls 1 dozen each and salmon and paste sandwiches. They also purchased 30 cigarettes and various sweets to hand round. The cost of the party was £9 and a great success.

At this time members were having two outings during the summer and a visit to the pantomime at Christmas. Also meetings were being held at the Vicarage once a month during the winter months as the hall was too cold. Mrs Eddington was Chairman at this time. In 1965 there were 17 members who went to the pantomime and enjoyed it very much.

Pictures of members appeared on the television.

AGM Feb 1967
Mrs Eddington gave an update on New Village Hall [she was on the Parish Council]. The fund is now £1,046. And the lease has now been signed. We have now got to fence the ground.

That Christmas Mr Rampton gave a very generous cheque for £10 to the club. It was decided to give each member 10s. as well as their ¼lb of tea. Colton Good Companions closed in December 1969 and members were invited to join Easton and four joined.

The New Hall was opened in 1969 and at that time the club had 21 members. But it seems the rent in July 1971 was a bit too high, 40p for each meeting. The club said the most they could afford was 25p. The Village Hall committee decided that they could have it rent-free for their meetings and this went on for several years. At this time subscriptions were put up to 20p for a year or 10p half yearly.

AGM 1975
It was decided to hold meetings twice a month now, on the first and third Thursday of the month. The Club went through a rough patch that year and had to ask the Chairman [not Mrs Eddington] to resign as there was so much bad feeling.

After this, in 1976, Mr Percy Buxton was elected chairman and this position he held until 1988. Things went much better, there were more outings and he arranged a summer holiday most years. For this they had a savings fund that Doris Blogg used to run. Jean Ditton resigned at the beginning of 1977 after being secretary for 12 years but she soon came back and was secretary for another 15 years until 2002.

Right: Left to right: *Hilda Greenacre and Ellen Gent, 1980s.*

Below: Left to right: *Mr and Mrs Greenacre and Ellen Gent, c.1986.*

Above: *Good Companions' holiday, 1980s.*

Right: *Victorian fête with the Good Companions, 1987.* Left to right: *Ellen Gent, Joan Chapman, Maggie Lee (holding baby Sarah), Helen Mortimer.*

Below: *Meal in the Village Hall for the Good Companions and guests, 1980s.*

Good Companions' outing to Flatford Mill, 1980s.

AGM 1980
The Royal Norfolk Show tickets would be £2.50 first day and £2.00 second.

AGM 1982
Marlingford Club has now finished – the possibility of having extra members in our Club was discussed. At present there is only one Marlingford person able to get to Easton so it was agreed that Mrs Simms would be welcomed to come to our Club. This will bring our membership up to 34. It was agreed that a limit on the membership should be 36 and then there would have to be a waiting list.

In 2004, after all these years, Mrs Simms, Betty to all of us, is still a member. We have several valued members who live in Marlingford and the limit has now risen to 45. Some members come from Bawburgh and Honingham, two come from Hethersett, one from Easton and Olive Ward – a very active 95 year old – comes from Weston Longville.

Things have changed a bit now but we still have a very happy club. We have a fête in August, usually with a theme, to help with finances and Mr Rampton has helped us with his kind donation each year since 1967. This has been a great help allowing us to have a trip out most months and also to treat the members to a meal on the club's birthday and at Christmas. Mr Rampton has been very generous and helped with many organisations in the village

The Good Companions have achieved many things, one being the Quest Certificate awarded by Age Concern for introducing new activities. We have also run computer lessons and keep-fit classes.

The programme for 2002 was as follows: in March we had speaker Peter Ogden with 'Verse and Worse' which was very funny, and also a mystery trip to St Ives. For the Easter meeting we had a competition for the best Easter bonnet or buttonhole, and in April there was a trip to Langham Glass and Sheringham. In May we visited Ingarmells Market and Skegness. June is our birthday month and we had lunch at Yaxham Mill and later went to Felixstowe. July saw visits to Stamford and Belvoir Castle and in August we had our golden jubilee fête and a trip to Wisbech and Elton Hall. In September we went to Lowestoft and Somerleyton Hall and in October we had our harvest festival and gave members a tea. We also visited Bury St Edmunds. In November we had a Christmas shopping trip to Lincoln, which was very popular and, as ever, saw a full bus. In the same month we went on another day to Harry Ramsden's in Yarmouth for lunch and stopped at the Highways Nursery on our way home. At the beginning of December we went to the Highwayman at Winterton for lunch and Christmas entertainment. Then we had our Christmas party at which everyone received a present and we had a musical afternoon with games. The festivities continued with mince pies, Christmas cake and drink.

In January we went for a belated Christmas lunch at The Bell. In between all this we still have two meetings a month. It is not all bingo and whist by any means and we try to go out as much as possible. This is hard work for the committee as we are all getting older, but it keeps us busy.

I hope that there are many years left in this club yet. I know there will be changes and as the village gets bigger we hope new blood will come in. In Mr Buxton as chairman I had a very hard act to follow, but 15 years later I'm still there.

Above: *At the Good Companions fête in 1987 the theme was nursery rhymes.*

Left: *Father Christmas at the Good Companions, 1995. Left to right: Jean Ditton, George Stevenson, Joan Chapman.*

Below: *An outing with the Good Companions Club, 1992. Left to right: Vera and Alan Richards, Lucy and Horace Womack and Betty Mew.*

Above left: *An outing to Sandringham for the Good Companions, 1995. Left to right: Joan Chapman, Maggie Lee, Dot Everson, Doris Blogg, Keith and Lucy Rix, Pat Wiepen.*

Above right: *Olive Ward, the oldest member of the Good Companions' Club, at Somerleyton, 1997.*

Above: *Good Companions' outing to Sandringham, 1990s. Left to right: Edith Cocks, Gladys Betts, Maggie Lee, Brenda Bell, Joan Chapman, Pat Wiepen.*

Above left: *Pat Wiepen and Robbie Roberson at Chatsworth House, 1990s.*

Left: *Lunch outing with the Good Companions, 1993.*

Above: *Good Companions celebrating VE Day, 1995. Left to right, back row: Vera Richardson, Brenda Bell, Jean Ditton, Joan Chapman, front row: Pat Wiepen, Doris Blogg, Maggie Lee.*

Left: *Good Companions at the South Seas fête, 1998. Left to right: Margaret Van Jaarsveld, Jean Ditton, Clarice Kidd, Merilyn Cossey, Joan Chapman, Gladys Betts.*

Below: *Good Companions at the fête refreshment counter, 1990s. Left to right: Edith Cocks, Doris Blogg, Edith Kidd, Dora Fulcher.*

Above: *Good Companions Club on an outing to Leonardslea, 1996. Left to right: George Stevenson, Pat Wiepen, Joan Chapman, Merilyn Cossey, Gladys Betts, Herbert Roberson, Brenda Bell, Barbara Lenehan, Margaret Bailey.*

Left: *Revd Angela Reynolds at the best Easter bonnet Good Companions Club day, 1999.*

Below: *Christmas with the Good Companions; Father Christmas is George Stevenson, 1990s.*

Above: *Age Concern competition at the Royal Norfolk Show, 1997, showing how life was in 1947 and how it is today. The Good Companions won first prize.*

Left: Left to right: *Robbie Roberson and George Stevenson at Banham Zoo, 1990s.*

Below left: *Olive Ward, winner of the Easter bonnet competition, 1999.*

Below right: *Lunch at Sprowston Hall, Christmas 1993. Left to right: Joan Chapman, Jean Ditton, Brenda Bell.*

Above: *The committee's last Pop-In meeting before Christmas 2003. They met again in 2004.*

Top right: *Golden jubilee celebration cake, 2002.*

Right: *The church decorated for harvest festival, c.1980s.*

The Pop-In
by Wendy Dorr

The Pop-In first took shape at a coffee morning on Tuesday 1 May 2001 at 10a.m. in the Village Hall, and was set up by the Revd Angela Reynolds, Jean Ditton (secretary of the Good Companions) and Beryl Hillsdon (retired postmistress). When the Post Office closed its doors for good, the village lost its focal point and pensioners could no longer walk to collect their pensions as the nearest Post Office was two and a half miles away and not on a bus route. The Pop-In was a place for pensioners to sit and chat while waiting for a lift from the Community Car Scheme to take them to collect their pensions, and the younger mums came and helped to make the tea and coffee. We also held our regular monthly meetings with Post Office representatives at the Pop-In in our quest to reopen our Post Office.

In 2002 we decided to organise refreshments and table decorations for a tea party held after the golden jubilee Village Hall fête and Ann Dunbar made a special three-tier cake, in celebration of the jubilee. The party proved very popular, with a guest appearance being made by Dame Edna Everage, courtesy of Gordon Reynolds, complete with gladioli.

The Pop-In has continued to thrive as we have found more people are using the Post Office and stopping for a coffee and a chat. During the summer of 2003 a group of five first-year student nurses from the University of East Anglia called in. They had been given the village of Easton for their end-of-year community project. We were all happy to help with the answers to questions relating to what Easton could offer. They returned to take photographs around Easton and invited us to see their work on show at Hellesdon Hospital.

On Tuesday 8 July 2003 we were presented with a computer from John Lewis in Norwich which I won in a competition run by Age Concern. Peter Daynes provided us with a photograph of the village sign to use as a backdrop picture on the monitor screen and has put photographs of old Easton on file. Fred Creed has also archived photographs of the conservation work taking place at St Peter's Church.

Easton Table Tennis Club
by Eric Longbottom

The club began in the summer of 1982 when Easton entered a team in the South Norfolk Inter-Village Sports competition. One of the sports was table tennis and we raised a team of two senior players and two juniors. From this an interest developed. In 1983 a team called 'Startrite' was playing in the Village Hall but they were having difficulties raising a full team for every match. One of the players who lived in the village asked if he could help out and we soon found the necessary players. The following season, 1984/5, we changed the name of the team to 'Easton' and we have played under that name ever since. Our 20th anniversary as Easton Table Tennis Club will be celebrated in September 2004 and we still have players from our early years playing now! At present we have 12 registered players, two teams in the Norwich and District League, and we still play at the Easton Village Hall.

In the Vicarage grounds during the early 1930s. Left to right, back row: *Billy Smith, Bill Loseby, Jack Walpole, Tom Chapman, Barney Dade;* third row: *Ray Chapman, Archie Gent, Sam Kidd, Walter Scarfe;* second row: *Ernie Stone, Robert Scarfe, Donald Greenacre, Charlie Hart, Percy Blyth, Albert Middleton;* front row: *Victor Brand, Bertie Kidd, Jack Pratt.*

Laying the bowling-green, 1995/96. Left to right, back row: *Les Kid, Ken Trowse, Bill Baxter;* front row: *David Reynel, Brian Howe and Heriot Cossey.*

Right: *Charlie Earl, a founder member of Easton Bowls Club, at the opening of the new bowling-green, 1996.*

This image: *Bowls group outside the Vicarage, 1930s.*

Top: *Easton Bowls Club on opening day, 1996.*

Easton Bowls Club

Bowls have been played in Easton since the 1920s when a group of men bowled on the green behind the Church Room; if there was a special tournament arranged they might also play on the lawn at the Vicarage. Mr Charlie Earl – who kept the The Dog public house – decided with the help of all his friends to lay a bowling-green at the pub, and this they accomplished with a lot of hard work.

After 17 years of good sport the group was given notice to quit the green as the then pub owner wanted to apply for permission to build a 17-home housing development. The club then moved down to Marlingford Sports Club and started laying a new green. A working party was set up in September 1995 to clear an overgrown car park and after a lot of hard work the green was opened in May 1996 by Heddie Blyth, chairman of the Norfolk Bowling Association. The opening of the new club premises was a particularly special day for 79-year-old Charlie Earl, club founder and lifetime member, who had been landlord of The Dog for no less than 27 years.

Schoolchildren having a bad hair day, 2002.

Parent and toddler group having a teddy bears picnic, 2002.

Young gymnasts in the sports hall at Easton College, 2002.

Easton Gym Club

by Jo Tubby

The club was formed in 1984 with 18 gymnasts, no money, no equipment, one coach, one hour per week and Easton Village Hall as the only possible venue. Over the years the club has had to overcome many difficulties, but has always succeeded and become stronger. We have had champions in Norfolk and have won medals at competitions. At the time of writing we have over 100 gymnasts and seven qualified coaches, numerous assistants and helpers – all of whom give their time voluntarily. The driving force at present is Bradley Thompson who has moved the club forward to such an extent that we have a waiting list and can hardly cope with demand. We have our own website and have over £50,000 worth of equipment. Trophies, medals and certificates are awarded at our annual displays. In 2004 we celebrated our 20th birthday with a very special display in March.

Easton Junior Football and Netball

by Jo Tubby

Established in the 1980s at the request of my children, this group was conceived as little more than a few children playing with a ball! Due to its popularity, however, it has developed to become a club run by many helpers – and thanks to Youth Clubs UK we have been able to insure everyone (a necessary requirement these days). We would love to expand and play competitively but that remains a dream until we have our own pitches/courts in Easton. We have produced a county netballer and junior footballers have been selected to go to Norfolk/Norwich trials. We have a 17-year-old female qualified football coach and qualified netball coaches and umpires. Nearly all junior players have at some time been selected to play for their school.

Jo Tubby

Jo Tubby has lived in Easton for many years with her husband and two children. She is a keen sportswoman who plays tennis and hockey, the latter for the county. For many years she has believed that the children in the village should be able to enjoy sport, and set about establishing the facilities to enable them to do so, organising a junior football team and both a junior and adult netball team.

In the early 1980s Jo started Easton Gym Club, which enjoys an enviable reputation throughout the county and a highly qualified team of coaches. Through many difficulties with availability of venues, shortage of funds and sometimes low membership figures, Jo has always shown the determination and tenacity to keep things going. Many young adults from the village have enjoyed the benefits of Jo's dedication to sport. She is also an active member and supporter of the ongoing project to provide a new Village Hall in Easton and therefore better recreational facilities for the residents.

Easton Football Team with the Shoe Trades Cup, May 2003. Left to right, back row: Michael Cossey (secretary), Danny Barnes, Simon Rix, Stephen Shaw, Bob Stangroom, Martin Clarke, Eddie Jack (manager), Simon Rushforth, Colin Fell (sponsor), Andrew Jordan; front row: Rory Perry, Neil Baxter, Tim Wickham, Neil Boyce, Spencer Laborde, Tom Payne, Matthew Rushforth.

Members of local football teams, 2002.

Easton Football Club

Football has been played in Easton for many years. In the 1950s there was a football pitch behind The Dog, where there were mainly friendly matches played against local villages. Later, in the mid-1960s, a piece of land was made available for a new football pitch, by landowner Mr J.M. Rampton on Dereham Road, opposite the junction of Bawburgh Road. There were many hours spent by local people including Ben Harrowven, Ray Jenkins, John King, Roy Mortimer and Gordon Rudd to prepare the pitch in readiness for Easton FC's first attempt at playing competitive league football. This happened in the 1967/68 season when the club affiliated to Norfolk County Football Association and joined the Norwich and District Football League.

In 1974 the club decided to change leagues and joined the Norwich Business Houses Football League, which is where the club's two teams are playing at the time of writing.

In the 1980/81 season the club reached their first cup final, the F.J. Potter Cup, which they unfortunately lost to Wensum FC. The club re-formed the reserve team, managed by Peter Caton, in the 1983/84 season.

The pitch on Dereham Road was home to Easton FC for nearly 30 years, but when it became apparent that it was to be lost to a housing development, the club were forced to move to keep the facilities required by the league. The club moved just down the road to Marlingford Sports Club for about four years, then found a more permanent home at Easton College. Mr Rampton then provided another piece of land, again on the Dereham Road, which is the proposed site of the new Village Hall and Sports Field – perhaps history will turn full circle?

The first team gained promotion to Division One in the mid-1980s and has remained in the top division to this day. The team has always been competitive, but had to wait until the 2002/03 season to gain their first piece of silverware, reaching the Shoe Trades Cup Final against Earlham Bridges. It was played on 1 May 2003 at Mulbarton FC. After a close match which finished 3–3 after extra time, Easton won on penalties. The Shoe Trades Cup was first competed for in 1929 and is an impressive trophy which Easton were proud to win.

The club has been blessed with local football enthusiasts who have given loyal, valuable service. Past chairmen include Mr Peacock and John King,

with Alan Hewitt taking over in 1979 to the time of writing. Past secretaries include Gordon Rudd, Ann and Ben Harrowven, Colin Fox (1976–81), Chris Clare (1981–85), passing over to Michael Cossey, the secretary in 2004. Freddie Rix ran the line for Easton for many years, and Graham Seely is still a valued linesman. Another loyal member was Bob Spinks who served the club in various capacities, too numerous to list, for over 20 years from the early 1970s to the mid-1990s. On the playing side, one name that stands out from the rest is Andrew Jordan, who played his first game at 14 years old in the 1978/79 season and is still playing at present, 25 years later. Last but not least, club president, Mr J.M. Rampton, has given valued support for nearly 40 years.

Above: *Easton Football Team, 1975/76.* Left to right, back row: *David Kidd, Ted Ward, Ben Harrowven, David Vogt (captain), Roberts Spinks, Alan Smith, Michael Barratt, Graham Webb, John Abel (manager);* front row: *Chris Clare, Paul Blyth, Anthony Ward, Colin Fox, Ray Jenkins.*

Below: *Easton Football Team, 1979.* Left to right, back row: *Joe Green (manager), Robert Spinks, Eddie Green, Willie Jeffreys, David Green, Paul Bingham, Terry ?, David Vogt (captain);* front row: *Colin Fox, Bob Green, Paul Franklin, Neil Phillips, Chris Clare, Andrew Adair.*

Street parties in celebration of the royal wedding of Charles and Diana, 1981. The events were organised by Easton Playgroup, along with supervisors and helpers, in Woodview Road and Kennedy Close.

Above: *Mothers and toddlers celebrating the royal wedding, Village Hall, 1981.*

Right: *Cover of Easton's programme for the Queen's silver jubilee.*

Silver Jubilee, 7 June 1977

The programme of village events for this royal occasion were as follows:

A. *Youth Football five-a-side Knockout Competition.*
 (Football field)
B. *Bowls Competition Part 1.*
 (Bowling Green, Easton Dog)
C. *Bowls Competition Part 2.*
D. *Ladies' and Men's Novelty Football Match.*
 (Jubilee Playing Field)
1. *Children's Sports.*
2. *Refreshments available in the Village Hall.*
3. *Decorated Cycle Competition.*
 (Jubilee Playing Field)
3.1 *Children's Jubilee Tea. (Village Hall Car Park)*
3.2 *Jubilee Draw and Presentation of Art Competition Prizes.*
4. *Bowls Competition Finals. Presentation of the Jubilee Trophy.*
5. *Jubilee Dance. (Village Hall)*

As the ladies were outnumbered in the novelty football match, some of the men dressed as women; one was a nurse and the hair on his chest didn't look right somehow! Two people were in charge of the big wet sponge and bucket and ran on at every opportunity to administer it. There was also a stretcher with just one nail attaching the canvas to the handles. This was laid down on the ground and the injured player was placed on it. It was then picked up and the bearers ran off with it leaving the injured person still lying on the canvas in the field! Everybody had a lovely day. The village sign was

designed and produced by Mr Harry Carter for the jubilee and as a further memento all children aged 16 and under on the day were presented with a silver jubilee crown.

The Parish Council gave £250 and donations also came from Mrs Steward, from a Bowls Club match (£5), from the jubilee draw (£79), and a disco dance (£26). This added up to a total of £381.08 to spend on the bunting, prizes, crowns, a party, dances and refreshments. And £52.19 was still left over – how prices have changed!

Royal Wedding

In spite of Easton Parish Council's announcement that parishioners would be too busy watching TV to organise other celebrations, the residents of Woodview Road and Kennedy Close had a street party to celebrate the wedding of Prince Charles and Lady Diana Spencer in 1981. Two cakes were made and decorated, one for Prince Charles and one for Lady Diana, by Pam and Paula Millwood. The heavily laden tables greeted the children after races on the Jubilee Playing Field. Balloons were on display and each child received a crown and a tin of toffees. Race winners also gained a windmill. Everybody enjoyed the day and Pam Millwood served teas from her front garden.

Members of the congregation of St Peter's Church gathered for a harvest picnic, 2002.

Workers on the allotments, 2002. Left to right: William Earp, Philip, George and Andrew Brockbank, John Walne, Muriel Pegg and Martyn Davey.

Chapter Nine

❧

The Modern Village

The completed 'Buxton Close' scheme, 1990.

The first action – erecting the site signboard, 1989.

Easton Self-Build Housing

In early 1989, with high interest rates and escalating house prices, South Norfolk District Council selected the old Airey council-house site on Marlingford Road to trial an initiative to provide affordable housing for young local people. The council approached young couples and individuals, who had placed themselves on the council-housing list, with the outline of the scheme. From those who expressed an interest and attended an interview 19 members were selected, eight from village families. These members formed Easton Self-Build Housing Association Limited. As the council could not know what level of experience to expect when the concept was originally born, a self-build management company was identified to manage the scheme. As it transpired only eight members worked in construction with others from industries as diverse as hairdressing and engineering. The scheme was designed by the Trevor Jolley Stanwick Design Partnership, funded by the Halifax Building Society, and the chosen bankers were the Royal Bank of Scotland, mostly as a result of their previous working relationships with the management company. From the initial interview meetings were held and the chairman, secretary and treasurer were duly elected. Although the management company would organise works across the whole site (roads, sewers, etc.), it was down to the individual members to arrange for the works to their own properties by employing subcontractors or doing the works themselves with the management company providing technical expertise.

Work commenced on site in April 1989 with the breaking up of the slabs left following the demolition of the Airey Houses and stripping back the topsoil. At that point the first of many problems arose when, in trying to set out the properties, it was not possible to orientate them correctly. As with all other problems thrown at the group of young people, this was overcome and foundations were soon being dug and concreted with members all helping each other.

Members mucking in to concrete foundations, 1989.

Work then progressed in earnest and soon the next major stumbling block arrived – no money! The management company had failed to ensure that a contract was in place. Individual members paid their individual subcontractors from their savings, although relationships with suppliers were fraught. The matter was eventually resolved and the association was able to pay suppliers and members when funds arrived in early November 1989. Progress from this stage was very good with members spending most of their spare time working on site – indeed The Dog did very good trade at this time as members would take time out most evenings for a pie and a pint on their way home.

Progress in March 1990.

The major threat to the scheme arrived in March 1990 when the management company went into receivership. The members bonded together and, after negotiations with the funding body, the scheme progressed with Mick Flatt and his partner Trudy Brooks, both of whom worked in construction, providing the management and accounting skills to complete the project. The project was one of 11 that the management company was working on and the association members should take great pride from the fact that this was the only scheme which was completed. Work on individual properties progressed and several 'site working' days were also arranged, when topsoil was placed and levelled, fencing installed and erected, and the members had great fun.

Digging the footings, 1989.

Clearing the site, 1989.

The scheme progressed and a date was set for the 'buy out', when the members purchased the individual properties from the association. On 30 October 1990, 19 young individuals and couples became proud owners of their own 'dream home'. At this time South Norfolk District Council arranged their own celebration and on 19 October 1990 the then Member of Parliament for South Norfolk, the Right Honourable John MacGregor, was invited to open the scheme.

John MacGregor (left) with ESBHA chairman Mick Flatt (right), 1990. Also present are the council chairwoman and Mr M. Goodsen from SNDC.

To celebrate the event and also to thank the village, which had been very supportive of the scheme, an open day was organised for Saturday 3 November 1990. The day commenced with Mrs Buxton cutting a ribbon to commemorate the naming of the close – 'Buxton Close', after her late husband Mr Percy Buxton, a parish councillor who had devoted much of his life to the village. Throughout the day an 'open house' was operated on the scheme and villagers were invited to view the properties. In the evening a firework display and bonfire were held, finishing with a celebration disco.

For some who had never encountered construction, undertaking the scheme alone would have been

Mrs Buxton names the close, 1990.

Mandy Fell (née Parsons) and Jenny Savage (née Hobson-Frohock) – two of the village youngsters to benefit from the Self-Build Scheme, 1990.

a daunting task, let alone the additional problems thrown at the association. The young members should take particular pride that they stuck at the project to completion. Indeed, the close almost became a 'community within a community' and many members have maintained contact even though they have moved up the property ladder.

Special thanks should go to South Norfolk District Council for the original scheme, although some disappointment must be expressed that only one other scheme was attempted by them. Perhaps in the future, with the rising cost of homes, local councils will again look at this option for local, low-income families. Thanks are due to Mr Mike Tomlinson, our local district councillor, who was always available when the going got tough, and to Halifax Building Society who stuck with us at a time of high failure amongst self-builders generally.

The scheme has enhanced the village and the association members in many ways and all who took part in the venture certainly learned something about themselves.

The members celebrate their achievement, 1990.

147

Opening of southern bypass, 1992.

Crowds gather at the new bypass, 1992.

New Bypass

The village has had the main Dereham Road altered many times, which was straightened and also flattened in places. The road was always very dangerous and there were many accidents and several deaths. The southern bypass was opened on Friday 11 September 1992, when the village was a much quieter and safer place to live. The cost to build the bypass was £100 million and it stretches for 14 miles, starting at Easton and leading towards Norwich. The road was officially opened by the then Transport Secretary John MacGregor, who cut the three ribbons in front of several hundred people. He then rode a short distance in a Norwich Union mail coach in front of a 30-strong cavalcade. One man was arrested after protesters halted the vehicles. The environmentalist staged a sit-down protest in front of an Anglian Water lorry and chained himself to its bumper with a cycle lock. There was also an accident, in which a Barford Hire truck overturned, but nobody was hurt. It was thought at the time that the bypass would be carrying up to 25,000 vehicles a day. Mr MacGregor predicted that traffic through Easton would be cut from 14,000 vehicles a day to 2,000. In 2004 plans for a northern bypass are in the pipeline.

When the bypass was opened the Dereham Road through the village was closed for a village party. Plates of cakes and sandwiches were provided for the children in the car park at The Rembrandt, which at that time was owned by the Clarkes. The church band provided the music, and a bouncy castle and clown amused the children. Mr John MacGregor addressed the crowd, as this road had been long awaited by the residents, and a good time was had by all, with dancing on the main road. The Dog public house served free drinks and bowls of chips.

Four views of the bypass, 2000.

Airey Houses, 1948–87

These were prefabricated houses built by H. Smith of Honingham for Forehoe and Henstead Council to house ex-servicemen after their demobilisation. There were five blocks of two built on Marlingford Road, made of concrete slabs on a steel and concrete frame with cedar shingles on the roof. They had three bedrooms and a bathroom upstairs and a kitchen and two reception rooms downstairs, with a toilet and wash-house outside. Joan Chapman recalls:

The living-room had a solid-fuel Rayburn cooker that heated the water and kept the whole house warm in the winter. It was lovely to cook on once you learned how to regulate the heat – there was no heat gauge, so you just used your hand to test the heat. We had nearly 40 happy years living at No. 28 – and although they were only built to last 20 years they survived a further 20. Towards the end of their time they were very draughty and the window-frames were bent with big gaps that the wind came straight through. They had big gardens and the ground was very stony.

At least half the resident families were moved over to Parkers Close, when a bungalow became empty. Buxton Close is now on the site where the Airey Houses once stood. Joan continues:

The fire service used the last two houses to demonstrate how fire alarms saved lives and how easy foam-filled furniture is set alight. A newspaper report stated that smoke alarms cost £15 each (quite expensive in 1987). Within 20 seconds of starting the fire in the living-room, by dropping a lighted match on the settee, the alarms went off. Within five minutes, flames and toxic black smoke was billowing out of the windows and the walls began to disintegrate. This was quite a thing to watch and it drew a big crowd.*

Left: *Playing in the snow outside the Airey Houses, 1960s. Left to right: Alan Wiepen, and Sheila and Sandra Chapman.*

Below and bottom: *Airey Houses being demolished, 1986.*

Above: *Looking towards Norwich, c.1999.*

Left: *A view of the houses pictured above being built, c.1999.*

Below: *An old view towards Dereham, c.1940.*

View of the road from the church end of the village, looking towards Norwich, before the road was straightened and widened, 1950s.

Looking towards the church. The far cottages are Rose Cottages, 1950s.

New houses being built, c.1998, looking towards the church.

Houses being built next to the pub, c.1999.

The new housing estate being built on Bawburgh Road, early 2003.

❧ A Miscellany of Names and Faces ❧

Left: *Bertie and Hettie Mortimer, c.1930s.*

Below: *Family group at the wedding of Violet Scarfe and Tom Wright, opposite Rose Cottages in Easton, with Peggy Taylor (niece of the bride) at the front of the group, 14 May 1938.*

Bottom right: *Joan, Ted and Pat Gent, 1930s.*

Bottom left: *Daisy Scarfe as a bridesmaid to her sister Violet, 1938.*

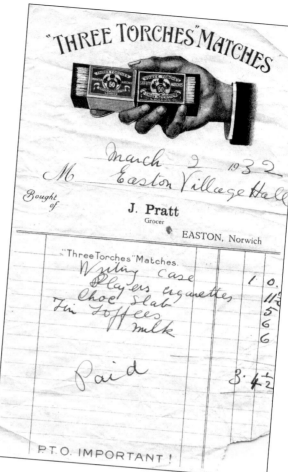

Above: Left to right: *Joan Gent, Hilda Peacock and Pat Gent, with Ida Barber standing, c.1938.*

Below: *Pat and Joan Gent with an American friend, called Charles, 1940s.*

The Mortimer family, early 1900s.

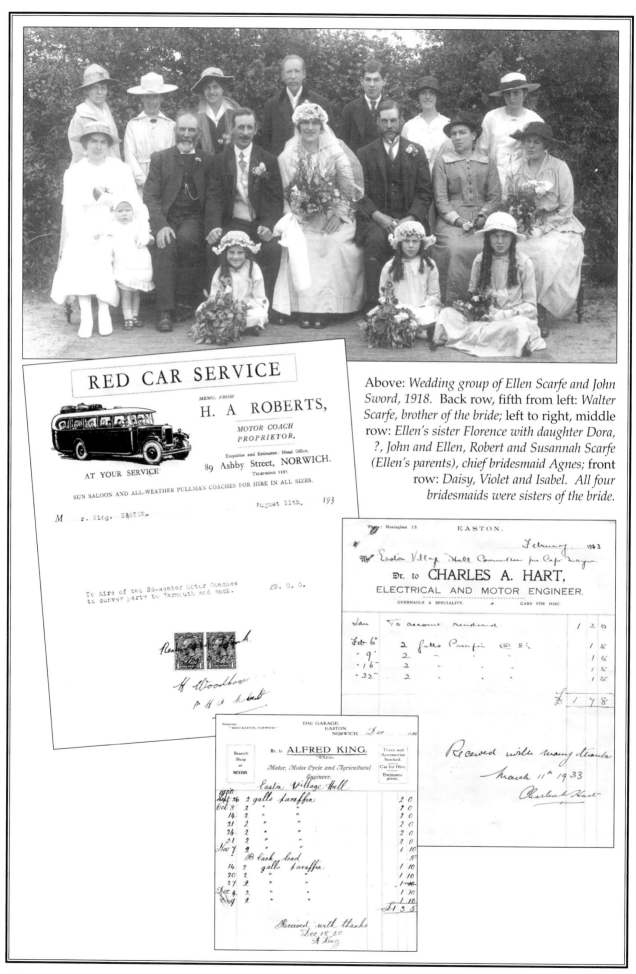

Above: *Wedding group of Ellen Scarfe and John Sword, 1918. Back row, fifth from left: Walter Scarfe, brother of the bride; left to right, middle row: Ellen's sister Florence with daughter Dora, ?, John and Ellen, Robert and Susannah Scarfe (Ellen's parents), chief bridesmaid Agnes; front row: Daisy, Violet and Isabel. All four bridesmaids were sisters of the bride.*

Above: *Easton Youth Club in the Church Room, during the late 1950s.*

The 'Pop-In' on Tuesday mornings between 10a.m. and 12 is a chance for villagers to meet and have tea and coffee in the Village Hall. The computer, pictured here in 2003, was won in an Age Concern competition and was donated by John Lewis.

Subscribers

Harold Howard Abel

C.J. and P.A. Adcock, Easton

Sandra J. Angelo (Chapman), Hethersett, Norfolk

Sylvia D. Balderstone, Stoke-Holy-Cross, Norfolk

Mr Basil Baldwin, New Costessey, Norfolk, grandson of Robert and Emily Hurrell

Mr and Mrs K.E. Balls, Norwich, Norfolk

V. Barber, Easton

Andrew Barker, Easton

Sylvia and Harry Barker, Easton, Norwich, Norfolk

Jane, John and Sarah Barley, Cringleford

Elsie Barnes (née Hawkes), formerly of Easton

Janice and David, Daniel, Emily Barnston, Easton, Norfolk

Adam D. Battley, Wymondham, Norfolk

Margaret A. Battley, Chapel Break, Bowthorpe, Norwich

Brenda and Rex Bell, Bawburgh, Norfolk

S. and S. Bennett

Neville and June Bird, Marlingford, Norfolk

John Blackburn, Sprowston, Norwich

Mary and Paul Blathwayt, Easton

John Bliss

Helen Ann Bloomfield (née Mortimer), Easton, Norfolk

The Bourne Family, Easton, Norfolk

Darren Brightwell, Easton, Norfolk

Lorraine Gent Burke, Edinburgh

Bream, Canham, and Carver Family, Easton, Norfolk

Mark and April Caton, Easton

Mr Peter Caton

Cheryl L. Chapman, Easton, Norfolk

John Chapman, Victoria, Australia

Roland T. Chapman, Easton, Norfolk

Irene Mary Clarke

Philip, Lisa, Holly and Erin Cooper, Easton, Norfolk

Mark and Jean Cordy, Easton, Norwich

Chris and Tracy Cossey, Easton, Norfolk

Michael J. and Jillian A. Cossey, Easton, Norfolk

Babs, David, Kimberley and Carly Cox, Easton, Norfolk

Linda and David Crowe, Wymondham, Norfolk

Mrs Jill Cushing (née Ottaway), originally from Colton

Jude Ditton

Peter Ditton

Robert Ditton

Wendy, Malcolm and Elizabeth Dorr, Easton, Norfolk

Amanda Fell, Easton, Norfolk

Mick and Trudy Flatt, Easton, Norfolk

June and Cedric Flood, Costessey, Norfolk

B. Frost, Easton, Norwich

Dian Frost (née Roberson), Lower Easton

Mrs Rosemary Frost, Taverham. Easton Press Reporter

Bernard and Jean Gaskin, Easton (1973–87)

Amanda Gent, Musselburgh, East Lothian

Christopher Gent, Musselburgh, East Lothian

Eddie and Irene Gent, Musselburgh, East Lothian

Sheila Goram (née Chapman), Hethersett/ Easton

Mr and Mrs P. Green, formerly of The Old School House, Easton

Ronnie Greenacre, Norwich, Norfolk

Margaret and Colin Hall, Easton, Norfolk

Mrs Janet Hanwell (née Dade)

Thomas J. Harrowven, Easton, Norfolk

Trevor G. Hart, Easton, Norfolk

Pam and Trevor Hedge, Bawburgh, Norwich, Norfolk

Mrs Thelma Hewitt, Thorpe St Andrew, Norwich

Pamela Hooker, Easton, Norfolk

Janet Howard (née Tuck), Wymondham, Norfolk

Mrs S. Howard, Bushby, Leicester

Alison and James, William and Charlotte Hurn, Easton, Norfolk

Clair Jordan and Huw Jones, Easton, Norfolk

Mrs Karin Keeble, Attleborough

John and Nicola Kerrigan, Easton, Norfolk

James Kidd

Mr and Mrs L. Kidd, Easton Norwich

Peter J. Kidd, Kenninghall, Norfolk

Phyllis M. Kidd, Easton, Norwich, Norfolk

Stuart Kidd

Joy Kilbourn (granddaughter of A. King), Easton

Fred and Virginia Killick, Easton, Norwich

Hilary Kisby – Headteacher, St Peter's Primary School, Easton, 1993–2002

Sonia and George Lawn, Easton, Norfolk

Mr David Lawrence, Easton College

Linda and Trevor Lee, Easton, Norfolk

Mrs Margaret E. Lee, Easton, Norfolk

Patricia Lee (née Tuck), Fleggburgh, Norfolk

Barbara Lenehan, Easton, Norfolk

David Martin Lewis, Lower Easton, Norfolk

Hilda Longbottom (née Peacock), Easton, Norfolk

Kathryn Longbottom, Easton, Norfolk

Peter and Jean Mace, Easton, Norfolk

Mr and Mrs I.A. Mackay and Family

E.M. Mason, (descendant of The Harrowvens of Easton)

Betty and Angelo Matteucci

Enzo Matteucci

Federica Matteucci

Paul Matteucci

Vera C. Matthews, Costessey, Norfolk

Heather, Lynda, Andrew, Craig Mattless, Easton

Poul McCadden

Trevor McCadden

Steve G. Medler, Easton, Norfolk

Daphne J. Middleton, Easton, Norfolk

Barry and Carol Millard, Easton, Norfolk

Peter Milliken, Easton, Norfolk

John Michael Mortimer, Norwich, Norfolk

Nigel D. Mortimer, Easton

Mrs Rose Motta, Norwich

David and Jill Munro, Kennedy Close, Easton

Mrs Margaret Murray, Scotland

The Norwich Diocesan Board of Finance Ltd

Oswald and Charles Oswick, Easton, Norfolk

Pauline M. Parsons, Easton, Norfolk

Eric Peacock, Thorpe, Surrey

Stephen Peacock, Easton, Norfolk

Mr L.J. Pearson, Easton, Norfolk

Peter and Vivienne Pease, Easton, Norfolk

Stephen J. Pease, Toftwood, Norfolk

Timothy J. Pease, Easton, Norfolk

Muriel and Andrew Pegg, Easton, Norfolk

Joanne and Steve Proudfoot, Easton, Norfolk

Robert and Pamela Pyer, and Thomas and Florence Woodhouse, Easton

Clementine Rampton, Easton, Norfolk

Matthew and Katie Rampton, Easton, Norfolk

Thomas Rampton, Easton, Norfolk

Nicola J. Roberts, Aylsham, Norfolk

P. Roberts, Easton, Norfolk

Jan and Tony Robinson

Mrs A. Ruck, Wymondham, Norfolk

J.A. Savage, Ringland, Norwich

Arthur Scarfe, Easton

Peter Scarfe, Cringleford, Norwich

Scarfe, Sharp, Earl and Kidd, Easton

Dianne M. Scott, Blofield Heath, Norfolk

Dorothy and Richard Scott, Bowthorpe, Norfolk

Valerie Seaman, Easton, Norfolk

Graham and Margaret Seely, Easton, Norfolk

William Sharp, Easton, Norfolk
Ivan R. Shingles, Easton, Norfolk
Allan and Bessie Simkin, Hethersett, Norfolk
Mrs Betty Simms
Gillian Smith (née Cossey), Norwich
St Peter's Church of England VC Primary
  School
T.G., J., and J.I. Stanford, Easton, Norwich
Mr and Mrs Stork and Harry Stork, Easton
Helen D. Symonds, Little Melton, Norfolk
Gillian Taylor (née Chapman), Stokesby,
  Norfolk
D.S. Town and A.D. Merrell, Easton, Norfolk
John M. Tubby, Easton, Norfolk
Mary and Leslie Tuck, Easton, Norfolk

Peggy P. Tucker, Easton, Norfolk
Mrs Margaret van Jaarsveld, Easton, Norfolk
John F.W. Walling, Newton Abbot, Devon
Colin Walpole, Wacton, Norfolk
Olive Ward, Hethersett, Norfolk
The Wheelers, Easton, Norfolk
Michael Wiepen
Vivienne Wiepen
Mrs Dolly Wilkinson, Norwich
Ann Williams (née Richmond), Berkshire
Colin Winsor, Lowestoft, Suffolk
Margaret and Martyn Woodroffe, Warrington
Jean Youngs (née Fox), Norwich – born in
  Easton
Marco and Colette Zasiura, Easton, Norfolk

There are now over 120 titles in the Community History Series.

For a full listing of these and other Halsgrove publications, please visit
www.halsgrove.co.uk or telephone 01884 243 242.